Catherine Grady Crabtree

`ALA

SEATTLE

RESTAURANT RECIPES

RESTAURANT REVIEWS:
JANE EGGER
CHRISTINE MEINHART

RECIPES TESTED BY:
J & L CATERING

COVER AND RESTAURANT ILLUSTRATIONS:
LINDA WEBSTER

Printed in the United States of America
Published by Crabtree publishing
P.O.Box 3451
Federal Way, Washington 98003

For additional copies write directly
to Crabtree Publishing
or use order forms in back of book.

I.S.B.N. 0-937070-08-4

II

For Jonathan,
My dear little
sous chef.

Acknowledgements

A special thank you to the following:

Rich Beitlich, Julie Booker, Patty Cufley, Ray & Lynne Schow, Mary Puncochar, Marty VanPerre, Don Austin, Rick Randall, Michele Shaw, Jan & Jerry Ward, Katherine Davenport, Mona Grady, and the top 40 restaurants of Seattle.

Notes From Test Kitchen
by
Jane Egger

In the 20 years I've lived in the Seattle area, the restaurant scene has changed immensely. Dining out used to mean dark steak houses, deep fried seafood or Polynesian food, hardly anything to excite a gourmet's palate.

Now Seattle area chefs are world renowned and food trends begin here and head to other places. Our chefs are leaders in the new American cooking that specializes in the use of fresh regional ingredients presented in exciting imaginative ways. Visitors to Seattle are as enthralled by our restaurants as they are enthusiastic about Mt. Rainier, the Puget Sound and our friendly people.

The restaurants featured here have submitted outstanding recipes for you to try. How about Salmon onBraised Lettuce and Herb Sauce, Roasted Chicken with Red Pepper Sauce, Fresh Ginger Ice Cream or Ginger Chicken Salad, a Steamer Bucket full of mussels, clams and scallops. These recipes and many more are in here waiting to be tried by you!

We have tested all these recipes, simplifying them when needed. Where seasonal ingredients are called for, we have made suggestions for substitutions so you may prepare the recipes year round. Terms unfamiliar are defined in the Glossary. Our desire has been to make these recipes family favorites, easy to prepare and fun to serve. We want you to reach for this cookbook when you think about a memorable meal or when you just want something easy but unusually delicious for you and your loved ones. Enjoy using A LA SEATTLE. We think it will soon be your favorite cookbook.

Table of Contents

Table of Contents - continued

Adriatica

ADRIATICA
CUCINA MEDITERRANEA

Approaching the villa-styled home overlooking Lake Union and contemplating its name evokes images of romantic fishing ports on the Adriatic Sea. You can find restaurants on the Adriatic where local fishermen not only bring in the day's catch (imagine the splendor of piles of mussels, squid and fish of every sort) but eat there as well.

The Adriatica restaurant is a touch of this and much more, bringing you a taste of its namesake and origins with such delicacies as fried squid with skordalia (considered the best in Seattle), Prawns Skiathos with Linguine, marinated grilled lamb, and steamed mussels rich with savory herbs and garlic.

For a lighter meal and more casual atmosphere, stop by the third floor view bar for a before - game or after theatre appetizer or dessert.

1

The romantic atmosphere is punctuated by the friendly, personal service. If you're looking for a great restaurant with true Mediterranean flavor, I heartily recommend Adriatica!

Adriatica is located at 1107 Dexter No., Seattle.
For reservations call 285-5000. Complimentary parking to the south of the building after 5:00 p.m.

ADRIATICA PRAWNS SKIATHOS WITH LINGUINE

A LA - Adriatica Cucina Mediterranea

1/2	**cup olive oil**
1-1/3	**cups onion** (minced)
1-1/2	**T. garlic** (minced)
2	**cups tomatoes** (peeled, seeded and chopped)
2/3	**cup dry white wine**
1/4	**cup lemon juice**
1	**t. crushed red chilies** (or more to taste)
1-1/2	**lbs. prawns or large shrimp** (shelled & deveined)
1	**lb. feta cheese** (divided into two, 1/2 lb. portions)
2	**T. fresh basil** (chopped) **or 1 t. dry**
1 - 1½	**lbs. fresh linguini** (or 8-12 oz. dried)
1/4	**cup parsley** (minced)

1. In a large saute pan, heat olive oil on high; add onion and garlic. Cook until soft but not brown.
2. Add tomatoes; cook for 1 minute; add wine, lemon juice, and chilies.
3. Reduce for about 1 minute.
4. Add prawns, 1/2 lb. of the feta and all of the basil. Cook until prawns are done and feta is creamy (about 3 minutes).
5. Meanwhile, cook linguine until Al Dente.* Drain and place on serving dish; pour sauce over.
6. Crumble the rest of the feta over the top, then sprinkle with parsley and serve.

Serves: 4-6
Preparation: 15-20 minutes

*See Glossary for *Al Dente.*

A wonderfully seasoned dish. Try over rice also.

3

ROASTED GARLIC WITH MONTRACHET AND CROUTONS

A LA - Adriatica Cucina Mediterranea

8	**heads garlic**
1/2	**cup olive oil**
1/4	**cup butter** (melted)
1/4	**cup water**
	sprinkle of any fresh or dried herbs such as; rosemary, basil, oregano or thyme
	thinly sliced baguettes (toasted until golden brown)
1/4	**lb. Montrachet Chevre cheese**
	tiny olives (garnish-optional)

1. Preheat oven to 275º.
2. Peel loose paper off garlic heads, leaving the cloves intact in casing. Cut 1/4" off the top of each head of garlic (not the root end).
3. Place in oven proof pan just large enough to hold garlic, with cut side up.
4. Pour olive oil, butter and water over the garlic. Sprinkle with herbs.
5. Cover pan tightly with foil.
6. Bake for two hours or until garlic is very soft and spreadable. Take garlic heads and squeeze out buttery-like spread and discard casings.
7. Serve warm, spread on baguettes and topped with thin slices of montrachet. Garnish with tiny olives if you wish.

Serves: 8 as appetizer
Preparation: 5 minutes
Baking: 2 hours

Try this appetizer as a different hors d 'oeuvre or first course for a special meal.

4

Benjamin's

Benjamin's

Follow the sailboats or your good taste to Benjamin's on Lake Union. You will find a restaurant that exudes Northwest "casual elegance". Cotton is as welcome as silk, polo shirts as welcome as jackets.

Add a dash of spice to the Northwest's bounty and you have the recipe for an open kitchen, bursting with action that's fun to watch from the eating bar.

For a more subdued experience, choose the elegant dining room away from the hum of chatter in the lively lounge. Or let the water, wind and sun enhance your dining pleasure on the open deck overlooking the lake and Seattle's hillside.

The Tortellini Alla Panna is a favorite; the salads seem gigantic; and the seafood is fresh, prepared to tender perfection. A very fine wine selection is available.

- continued -

A lively locale, a peaceful retreat: do we contradict ourselves? Alas, we find diversity. Come watch the ships; taste the wine and savor the seafood. The memory will stay etched in your mind for days to come.

Moorage is also available for our guests.

You'll find two locations at 809 Fairview Place North on Lake Union in Seattle, Call 621-8262, and 10655 Northeast 4th in Bellevue. Call 454-8255.

TORTELLINI ALLA PANNA

A LA - Benjamin's

18-24	**oz. veal-stuffed tortellini** (Italian Specialty Goods brand recommended or use your favorite brand)
1/4	**cup clarified butter***
1/2	**t. garlic** (peeled and minced)
1/4	**t. coarse ground black pepper**
1/4	**t. seasoning salt** (your favorite)
2	**canned artichoke hearts,** (cut into quarters)
1	**cup whipping cream**
1/2	**cup sour cream**
1	**cup Parmeson cheese** (divided)
3/4	**cup fresh spinach** (shredded)
1/4	**cup prosciutto ham** (minced)
1/4	**cup parsley** (chopped)

1. Pre-cook tortellini per package instructions and set aside and keep warm.
2. Heat butter, garlic and pepper in large frying pan.
3. Add tortellini and seasoning salt. Mix and taste for seasonings again. Add more if desired.
4. Add artichoke hearts and mix.
5. Add cream, sour cream and 1/2 cup of cheese. Mix well.
6. Add spinach and cook until cream thickens.
7. Place in serving bowl. Make stripes on top with parsley, the remaining cheese and prosciutto. Garnish with parsley sprig and serve immediately.

Serves: 4-6
Preparation: 20 minutes

*See Glossary for clarified.

Totally Fabulous! Combination of flavors is wonderful. Can be prepared ahead and served later for effortless entertaining.

9

LIME AND MINT VINAIGRETTE

(dressing for Grilled Shrimp next page)

A LA - Benjamin's

2-1/2	T. lime juice
1	T. dry mustard powder
2	T. mint leaves (minced)
1	pinch whole oregano
	dash of pepper
1	pinch of salt
1	t. red wine vinegar
1/4	t. fresh garlic (minced)
1/4	t. lemon pepper seasoning
1/3	cup salad oil

1. Combine all ingredients in bowl; mix well and refrigerate until cold.

Preparation: 5 minutes
Yield: about 1/2 cup

Great on Chilled Grilled Shrimp recipe on next page. Easy!

MINT

CHILLED GRILLED SHRIMP

A LA - Benjamin's

24	prawns, 21-25 per lb. size (peeled & deveined)
2	T. salad oil
1/4	cup or more of *Lime and Mint Vinaigrette* (see recipe previous page)
4	leaves radiccio or red leaf lettuce (garnish)
1/4	cup feta cheese (crumbled)
1	lime (cut into 4 wedges)
4	mint sprigs

1. Place prawns in small bowl; toss with salad oil and grill on BBQ, gas broiler or in oven under broiler until just done, about 2 minutes each side. **Do not** overcook.
2. Chill prawns in refrigerator for at least 1 hour. (Chill 4 plates at same time)
3. Place prawns in small bowl and toss well with the vinaigrette.
4. Place radiccio or red leaf lettuce on chilled plate. Place 6 prawns in front of garnish. Top with feta cheese and place lime wedges and mint sprigs to side of prawns.

Serves: 6 as 1st course salad
Preparation: 15 minutes (add 15 minutes if you have to peel and devein shrimp)
Refrigeration: 1 hour

A beautiful and delicious salad that's so easy and elegant! My guests raved! Yuppie, Yuppie, Yuppie!

PRAWNS AND STIR FRIED VEGETABLES

A LA - Benjamin's

4	**T. butter** (clarified*)
24	**prawns** (peeled and deveined)
1	**t. garlic** (peeled and minced)
1	**t. ginger** (peeled and minced)
20	**pea pods** (stems removed)
1	**cup celery** (bias cut)
1	**cup red peppers** (cut julienne*)
3/4	**cup white onions** (cut julienne*)
1/2	**t. seasoning salt**
1	**cup mushrooms** (sliced)
2	**T. lemon juice**
2	**T. white wine**
2	**T. soy sauce**
1	**tomato** (cut in 4 wedges)
1	**T. sesame seeds** (toasted)
1/4	**cup green onions** (bias sliced)
	parsley sprigs & lemon wedges (garnish)

1. Heat butter in frying pan; add prawns and cook until they slightly curl. Add garlic and ginger.
2. Add pea pods, celery, red peppers and onions, seasoning salt and cook 1 minute. Stir frequently.
3. Add mushrooms; season again and cook only to heat.
4. Add lemon, wine, soy sauce; blend well and cook 1 minute. Add tomato wedges; heat and serve on plate.
5. Top with sesame seeds and green onions. Garnish with parsley sprig and lemon wedge.

Serves: 4
Preparation: 30 minutes

*See Glossary for clarified and julienne.

Very colorful and very good!

BRAVO

Not just "bravo" but a standing ovation for Dorene Centioli Mc Tigue for seeing her wish come true, to give us a good Italian restaurant on the East Side. Located just off the busy 520 interchange, Bravo appears like a mirage from the east as you escape the highway hassles. A red tiled roof, tall pillars and brick paved entrance convince you of its authenticity. The moment you enter, an oasis of soothing sights, sounds and aromas will greet you.

An absolutely immaculate kitchen is in full view, where creative young chefs deftly caress pizza dough to smooth saucer-like perfection, shape pastas and grill fresh Northwest fish.

Something of which they are extremely proud at Bravo's is the wood-burning oven. The first of its kind in the Northwest, it produces mouthwatering pizzas and appetizers to rival any of the cities of Italy:

For a memorable lunch or dinner, escape to Bravo at 10733 Northup Way, Bellevue. Phone 827-8585.

MINESTRONE SOUP

A LA - Bravo

2/3	**cup olive oil**
2	**stalks celery** (chopped)
1/3	**lb. green beans**
1	**cup white onion** (chopped)
2	**carrots** (chopped)
1	**potato** (chopped)
1	**white turnip** (diced)
1	**(28 oz.) can tomatoes** (drained and broken)
3	**qts. chicken stock**
	combined in cheesecloth:

	3	peppercorns
	1/3	t. thyme
	1/3	t. basil
	3	bay leaves

1	**bunch fresh spinach**
1	**cup cabbage** (chopped)
1	**zucchini** (sliced)
	salt & pepper (to taste)

1. In large stock pot, heat olive oil and saute celery, beans, onions, carrots, potato and turnip. Leave crisp.
2. Add tomatoes, chicken stock and Spice Bouquet*. Bring to slow boil.
3. Add spinach, cabbage and zucchini and cook for 30 minutes or until vegetables are tender. Discard Spice Bouquet.
4. Season to taste with salt and pepper.

Serves: 6-8
Preparation: 1 hour

*To make Spice Bouquet: Place peppercorns, thyme, basil and bay leaves in cheese cloth pouch & tie with string to secure.

A rich variety of vegetables, nicely combined. Test kitchen liked this version of perennial favorite.

14

FETTUCCINE GORGONZOLA

A LA - Bravo

2	cups heavy cream
1	cube unsalted butter
2-1/2	oz. fresh, salted, shelled pecans
8	oz. imported Gorganzola cheese
1	lb. fresh egg fettuccine pasta
2	oz. Pancetta (Italian bacon) or any bacon (cooked crisp and crumbled)

1. Place cream and butter in saute pan over low heat.
2. Increase heat and bring to boil. Lower heat to simmer and cook until cream reduces in half.
3. Add pecans to cream; let soften.
4. Add cheese and whip with whisk to dissolve. Cook until mixture thickens. Meanwhile cook pasta (about 1-1/2 minutes for fresh), or according to directions. **Don't overcook**. Drain well. **Don't rinse**.
5. Place sauce in medium bowl; add pasta. Toss & garnish with crisp pancetta bacon and serve immediately.

Serves: 4
Preparation: 20 minutes

Multo Buono!

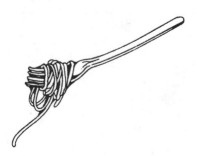

15

MONKFISH MEDALLIONS WITH ROASTED GARLIC CLOVES & CHIVE SAUCE

A LA - Bravo

10-12	**oz. Monkfish**
	flour (to dust)
	salt and white pepper (to taste)
1/4	**cup olive oil**
1/2	**cup dry white wine**
1	**cup fish stock*** (or canned clam juice)
1/2	**cup whipping cream**
12-16	**large roasted garlic cloves**
1/4	**lb. butter** (softened)
1	**bunch chives** (chopped)

1. Trim Monkfish and slice on the bias into 2oz. pieces. Dust with flour and season with salt and pepper. Set aside.
2. Heat olive oil in small saute pan to 220º; carefully add fish; lightly brown (30-60 seconds on each side). (Do Not overcook). Remove fish and keep warm in oven.
3. Discard excess oil and deglaze** pan over medium heat with white wine. Continue to cook until almost dry.
4. Add one cup fish stock*; reduce by cooking to half the portion.
5. Add half cup heavy cream along with roasted garlic cloves. Reduce by cooking until sauce thickens.
6. Remove from heat; add softened butter and whisk until butter dissolves.

- continued -

7. Remove garlic cloves and add chopped chives and salt and pepper to taste.
8. Remove fish from oven; pour sauce into platter; lay fish on sauce; garnish with garlic and additional chives.

Serves: 2
Preparation: 35 minutes

*Fish Stock: See Glossary
**Deglaze: See Glossary

A super delicious solution to preparing this area fish. Sauce could be used on any white fish. Be sure to try it!

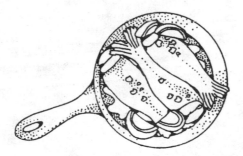

17

C.I. Shenanigan's

Many Seattleites and tourists alike are taking a fresh look at Tacoma and its new surge of beautiful waterfront restaurants. C. I. Shenanigans, overlooking Commencement Bay, is one such haven, just two miles from the busy port of Tacoma.

Beauty here goes beyond the rich cherry and walnut woodwork and breathtaking views. You'll be pampered by a friendly staff, and enjoy splendidly prepared cuisine with a choice of excellent wines. Munch on scrumptious appetizers at the seafood bar until 12:30 a.m.; relax in the piano bar or soak up the sun on the outdoor dining decks while your boat is moored at the private dock. This is the place in Tacoma for dancing up an appetite in the Video Club Rio (open nightly with a free buffet) or having a business lunch or a family Sunday brunch.

Though many come for the fine dining, you know with a name like Shenanigans you'll be in for a fabulous fun-filled time.

C.I Shenanigans is located at 3017 Ruston Way, Tacoma. Call 752-8811 for reservations.

DUKE OF WINDSOR SANDWICH

A LA - C.I. Shenanigan's

Curried Mayonnaise
1   cup mayonnaise
1/2   t. curry powder
1   t. lemon juice
3   drops tabasco sauce

Sandwich
2   slices sour dough bread
1   oz. bottled chutney sauce
4   oz. sliced turkey
1   lettuce leaf
2   slices fresh or canned pineapple

Curried Mayonnaise
1.   Mix together all ingredients for mayonnaise until well blended. Refrigerate in air tight container until you're ready to make sandwich.

Sandwich
2.   Place bread on cutting board.
3.   Spread 1 slice with Curried Mayonnaise; the other slice with chutney.
4.   Place lettuce on mayonnaise side; place turkey on chutney side; place pineapple on top of turkey.
5.   Put halves together and secure with wooden picks. Garnish plate with fruit and parsley.

Makes: 1 sandwich
Yield: 1 cup Curried Dressing
Preparation: 5 minutes

A new fresh answer to your sandwich doldrums.

20

HOT SEAFOOD PASTA SALAD

A LA - C.I. Shenanigans

4	T. butter
1	lb. scallops
2	cups mushrooms (sliced)
1	cup onions (diced)
2	cups broccoli flowerettes
1	whole red bell pepper
1/2	cup black olives (sliced)
1	cup pea pods
1	lb. shrimp
16	oz. rotini pasta (cooked)
8	oz. Bernsteins Italian Salad Dressing
	salt and pepper (to taste)
4	oz. parmesan (freshly grated)
	parsley (chopped-garnish)

1. Have all ingredients ready.
2. Place butter in large, hot saute pan.
3. Cook scallops, mushrooms, onions and broccoli until almost done, about 8-10 minutes.
4. Add bell pepper, olives, pea pods and shrimp and toss.
5. Add rotini, Bernsteins dressing and salt and pepper to taste.
6. Garnish with grated parmesan and parsley and serve immediately.

Serves: 6
Preparation: 20 minutes

This dish makes a beautiful presentation. Serve on a lovely platter. Your guests will think you're fantastic and the meal couldn't be simpler.

21

CHICKEN ALMOND SALAD

A LA - C.I Shenanigans

2	**boneless, skinless chicken breasts** (cut into 1" cubes)
3	**T. soy sauce**
1	**t. granulated garlic** (or 1 clove minced)
1/4	**cup butter** (melted)

Ginger Dressing
1/2	**cup apple cider vinegar**
1	**cup sugar**
1/4	**cup fresh ginger root**(peeled and minced)
1/2	**T. salt** (or to taste)
1-1/2	**cups salad oil**
3	**T. sesame seeds**

1	**small head green leaf lettuce** (torn into bite-sized pieces)
1	**cup celery** (diced)
2	**T. sesame seeds** (toasted)
1/2	**cup almond slices** (toasted)
4	**tomato wedges** (garnish)
4	**lemon wedges** (garnish)

1. Saute chicken in soy sauce, garlic and butter for 10-15 minutes until done. Drain. Set aside.

Ginger Dressing
2. Combine vinegar, sugar, ginger and salt in blender. Blend 5 minutes.
3. Pour oil in slowly while blending another 5 minutes.
4. Stir in sesame seeds by hand.

- continued -

Assembling Salad

5. Combine lettuce, celery, seeds, almonds and chicken in bowl.
6. Pour Ginger Dressing over and toss. Divide into 4 bowls and garnish with tomato and lemon wedges.

Serves: 4
Preparation: 25 minutes

A delicious favorite!

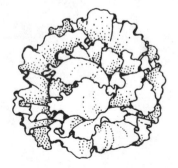

MUD PIE

A LA - C. I. Shenanigans

1	(8oz.) **box Nabisco Famous Chocolate Wafers**
1/3	**cup butter** (melted)
1/2	**gallon Mocha Almond Fudge Ice Cream** (softened)
1/2	**gallon Cookies & Cream Ice Cream** (softened)
	Hot Fudge Topping (heated)
	whipping cream
	sliced, toasted almonds

1. Put cookies in food processor to make crumbs. Combine with melted butter.
2. Press crumb mixture into bottom (not sides) of 9" pie plate. Freeze 1 hour.
3. Add softened Mocha Almond Fudge Ice Cream until it reaches top of pie pan. Freeze 1 hour.
4. Mound Cookies & Cream ice cream over top until center mound is about 6" high. (You will have some ice cream left over). Freeze again 1 hour or until ready to serve.
5. When ready to serve, ladle hot fudge on individual plates; place piece of pie; top with whipped cream and a sprinkling of toasted almonds.

Serves: 6-8
Preparation: 10 minutes
Freezing: 3 hours*

*It isn't necessary to freeze between each step but it makes removal from pie pan a little easier.

All Shenanigan fans will testify that this "Mile High Mud Pie" is the greatest! And it's EASY!

RASPBERRY SORBET

A LA - C.I. Shenanigans

1-1/3 lbs. raspberries (fresh or frozen)
1   lb. vanilla ice cream, premium quality (softened)
3   T. Creme de Cocoa liqueur
3   T. Amaretto liqueur
          whipped cream (garnish)
6   small mint leaves (garnish-optional)
6   small raspberries (garnish-optional)

1. Place all ingredients in blender or food processor and blend until smooth.
2. Portion mixture into 6 champagne glasses (6oz. per serving) and freeze several hours or overnight.
3. To serve: garnish with whipped cream. Place one berry in middle of cream and place small leaf next to it.

Serves: 6
Preparation: 5 minutes
Freezing: several hours or overnight

Beautiful; delicious with a taste of liqueur, and oh so easy!

The Alexis, a small hotel located in downtown Seattle, is renowned for its attention to detail and fine service in the best European traditions. Each guest is individually pampered.

It is only natural that a restaurant located in this hotel would exemplify these same principles. The Cafe Alexis is a small, 28 seat restaurant that seems polished and perfect in every detail, yet warm and gracious. It is the perfect place to enjoy an intimate, romantic meal.

The chefs at the Cafe Alexis use fresh ingredients both local and imported to give patrons dishes with an international flavor but simply presented. They like to have the food be as appealing to the eye as it is to the palate. The recipes they've chosen to share with us fit these criteria. Try the Smoked Salmon and Sorrel Tart for an easy but elegant brunch or finish your meal with a Plum and Black Walnut Tart or Fresh Ginger Ice Cream, guaranteed to become a family favorite.

The Cafe Alexis is located at 1007 1st Ave. in Seattle. For reservations, call 624-4844.

SMOKED SALMON AND SORREL TART

A LA - Cafe Alexis

1	(8") **pre-baked tart or pie shell**
6	**large sorrel* leaves** (stems removed, leaves thinly sliced)
4	**eggs**
2	**cups whipping cream**
1/2	**t. salt**
1/4	**lb. smoked lox salmon**
1/4	**cup creme fraiche**** or sour cream
2	**T. capers**

1. Preheat oven to 350º.
2. Spread sliced sorrel evenly in bottom of tart shell.
3. Beat together: eggs, cream, salt and pour into shell.
4. Bake in oven for 20 minutes or until set.
5. Remove; let cool for 5 minutes.
6. Arrange salmon slices over custard, covering completely.
7. Return to oven for 3 minutes to barely warm salmon. Do not let salmon cook or it will dry out.
8. Remove and drizzle with cream fraiche or sour cream.
9. Sprinkle with capers: serve immediately.

Serves: 8 as appetizer; 4 as light meal
Preparation: 25-30 minutes

* Sorrel is hard to find. You could substitute romaine or spinach or omit leaves entirely.

**See Glossary for *Creme Fraiche* recipe.

A test kitchen favorite. Flavors meld beautifully and complement. Very rich.

28

FRESH GINGER ICE CREAM

A LA - Cafe Alexis

2	**cups whipping cream**
2	**cups milk**
	3" piece fresh ginger root (coarsely chopped)
8	**egg yolks**
1	**cup sugar**
1	**t. vanilla extract**
1/4	**cup candied ginger** (finely chopped*)

1. Bring cream and milk to a boil.
2. Remove from heat; add fresh ginger.
3. Let ginger steep 30 minutes. Strain. Discard ginger.
4. Whisk together egg yolks, sugar and vanilla.
5. Add to warm gingered milk.
6. Return ingredients to saucepan over medium heat.
7. Cook, stirring constantly, until custard reaches 180º or coats a wooden spoon.
8. Chill mixture.
9. Freeze in any type of ice cream maker following machine directions.
10. Halfway thru freezing, add candied ginger.

Serves: 6-8
Preparation: 15 minutes
Steeping: 30 minutes
Freezing: several hours

* *Candied ginger* can be found in baking section of grocery store. It's put in fruit cakes also.

A wonderfully rich ice cream. Great with fresh fruit or sponge cake.

PLUM, BLACK WALNUT, COGNAC PIE

A LA - Cafe Alexis

2	**unbaked pie crusts to fit 9" pie shell**
2	**lbs. ripe Santa Rosa or Italian plums** (pitted and cut in eighths)
1	**cup sugar**
3	**T. cornstarch**
1/2	**t. salt**
2/3	**cup chopped black walnuts**
1/4	**cup cognac**
4	**T. butter**
1	**egg white**
2	**T. sugar**
	ice cream or whipped cream (for topping)

1. Preheat oven to 375º. Line 9" pie pan with one pie crust.
2. Combine plums, sugar, cornstarch, salt, walnuts and cognac. Mix.
3. Pour into pie shell.
4. Dot with butter.
5. Top with remaining pie crust. Crimp edges to seal.
6. Brush top with egg white and sprinkle with sugar.
7. Cut small slits in top crust.
8. Bake in 375º oven on bottom rack for 1 hour or until filling bubbles up through slits.
9. Serve warm with desired topping.

Serves: 6
Preparation: 10 minutes
Baking: 1 hour

Sure to delight all dessert lovers.

Café Dilettante

Take a breather from shopping at the Pike Place Market or come here intentionally to be tempted by the delectable chocolate treats.

You'll be greeted by rows of Chocolate Tortes, Chocolate Mousse, and Chocolate Decadence. Alas, Chocolate Heaven!

Waitresses out of a Renoir painting, and the sidewalk seating would have you believe you're in Paris.

Now you can become a "dabbler" in the art of chocolate confections by purchasing the elegantly packaged chocolates graced with the Dilettante rose to take home or give as gifts. Their rich flavor will leave an indelible mark on your palate.

Besides the finest espresso and cappuccino, Dilettante's has a hearty lunch repertoire with a fantastic Cabbage Carrot Borscht, other homemade soups, and fresh muffins to let you rethink Dilettante's as not "just a sweet place".

Cafe Dilettante is located at 1600 Post Alley, Seattle. Call 728-9144. Other locations:
Bellevue Square, 249 Bellevue Square, Bellevue. Call 455-4788. *Broadway Restaurant*, 416 Broadway E., Seattle. Call 329-6463. *1st Interstate*, 999 3rd., Seattle. Call 467-9593.

COCOA CAFE DELUXE

A LA - Cafe Dilettante

1/4	**cup hot espresso or coffee**
1/4	**cup hot chocolate***
1	**oz. Grand Marnier liqueur** (optional)
1/4	**cup foamed milk** (or more if desired)**
2	**T. whipped cream**

1. Combine coffee, hot chocolate and Grand Marnier in fancy cup or mug.
2. Top off with foamed milk and garnish with unsweetened whipped cream.

Serves: 1
Preparation: 3 minutes

*Dilletante uses their own brand of Hot chocolate called Ephemere.
**An espresso machine gives you foamed milk. If, like most people, you don't have one, beat hot milk with electric beater or put in blender.

A specialty at Cafe Dilettante. A good mocha flavor. Try on cool autumn evening or instead of dessert.

HOT CHOCOLATE

A LA - Cafe Dilettante

1 **cup Dilettante Ephemere Sauce** or other rich chocolate sauce such as fudge topping.
3 **cups milk (heated)**
1/2 **cup whipped cream (optional)**

1. Heat chocolate sauce slowly in sauce pan.
2. Pour sauce into heated milk.
3. Mix with a spoon. Pour into individual cups.
4. Serve warm with whipped cream if desired.

Serves: 4
Preparation: 5 minutes

Velvety smooth and rich.

RIGO JANCSI TORTE
Chocolate Torte

A LA - Cafe Dilettante

The Cake
1-1/4	**cups cocoa**
1/2	**cup flour**
1/4	**t. baking powder**
1/2	**cup whipping cream**
11	**large eggs** (room temerature)
1-1/2	**cups superfine granulated sugar**
2	**T. strong coffee or expresso** (very hot)

The Filling
2	**lbs. semi-sweet chocolate** or chips
2	**pints whipping cream**

The Glaze
12	**oz. semi-sweet or bittersweet chocolate**
1	**stick plus 1 T. unsalted butter** (cut into bits)

1	**11x17" jelly roll pan lined with waxed paper.**
1	**candy thermometer**

The Cake
1. Preheat oven to 350º.
2. Sift together: cocoa, flour and baking powder; sift together 2 more times. Set aside.
3. Whip cream in chilled bowl until smooth rounds form (not too stiff). Refrigerate.
4. Put 11 eggs in large mixing bowl and beat, first on low speed, then on high, until full volume is achieved. (Minimum of 15 minutes).
5. Gradually add sugar to the eggs in a slow stream, while continuing to beat.
6. Add the coffee. It should be very hot. This helps to set the eggs.

34

- continued -

7.   When the egg/sugar mixture is whipped to full potential, stop beating. Carefully fold in the flour/cocoa mixture.

8.   Fold in whipped cream.

9.   Pour the batter into the prepared jelly roll pan, making sure that it remains evenly distributed and level.

10. Place on middle rack, in oven, and bake for 30 minutes or until the cake is firm but slightly underdone. Start checking at 20 minutes.

11. Set the pan on a rack to cool. Do not remove waxed paper.

The Filling

1.   In a double boiler melt 2 pounds of finely chopped semi-sweet chocolate. Be sure no moisture or steam invades the chocolate. Stir constantly and do not let the temperature exceed 120º. Cool to 95º.

2.   Whip cream until soft smooth peaks form. (Not to stiff).

3.   Gently fold the chocolate into the cream to achieve a light, airy texture. Then whip for a few seconds more, being careful not to cause the cream to separate. The chocolate should incorporate smoothly into the cream. If the cream is too cold, and the chocolate too close to final set point, it will sometimes form little chunks, but that's all right. It makes an interesting texture.

To Assemble the Torte

1.   Cut cake in two and place one half on a serving plate. Remove waxed paper. Spread filling on top of this layer until the filling is smooth and even, approximately 1-1/2 inches thick.

2.   Chill in refrigerator until filling is firm.

- continued -

3.	Remove from refrigerator and carefully put the other half of the cake on top of the filling, peeling off the waxed paper in the process. (The cake is too tender to move without the paper on it).
4.	The cake is now ready to glaze.

The Glaze
1.	Break chocolate into small pieces and place in a double boiler. Melt, keeping moisture out. Do not let temperature go above 120º.
2.	Add the butter and beat the mixture until smooth and shiny.
3.	Cool slightly and pour over the top of the cake. Refrigerate until the entire finished torte is thoroughly chilled.
4.	Cut with a hot knife into pieces 2 to 3 inches square.

Serves: 10-12
Preparation: 1-1/2 hours
Baking: 30 minutes
Refrigeration: required between steps

Well worth the effort! Sinfully rich torte. A guaranteed hit!

The Rigo Jansci Torte is a specialty dessert from Cafe Dilettante reprinted here by permission of Harper & Row and Dana Davenport, author of "The Dilettante Book of Chocolates and Confections", Harper & Row, 1986.

CAFE JUANITA

An exciting restaurant whose popularity is spreading far from its Juanita base is Cafe Juanita. Italian food aficionados will revel in the authentic tastes emanating from this establishment's busy kitchen.

The pastas are fantastic and no wonder. They are fresh and hand-rolled daily (a true labor of love). Peter's many trips to Italy to observe eating and cooking styles are evident in the consistently careful presentations of wonderful food and wine.

In 1984 Peter started the Cavatappi Winery which produces some very fine sauvingnon blanc and muscat to enhance the already excellent wine list.

The sole with capers will melt in your mouth, and do savor the tender broiled lamb chops served with fresh steamed vegetables. Indulge in the luscious Walnut Torte or rich Gelato and/ or Crema D'Monforte; you can always take a stroll in the lovely garden to justify it.

Cafe Juanita is located at 9702 NE 120th Place, Juanita (Kirkland). Call 823-1505 for reservations.

CROSTINI
(Chicken Liver Pate on toast)

A LA - Cafe Juanita

2	**T. butter**
1/2	**onion** (chopped)
1	**lb. chicken livers**
	sage (to taste)
4	**T. capers** (or to taste / budget)
	salt and pepper (to taste)
2	**loaves French bread** (thinly sliced)
	olive oil

1. Melt butter in pan over medium heat and lightly brown onion. Add livers and saute 3 minutes; add 1 tablespoon water to pan; cover and lower heat. Cook additional 7 minutes or just until done and livers are just slightly pink inside.
2. Add sage - remember, fresh is much stronger than dried.
3. Remove liver and onions from pan and drain thoroughly. Let cool and put in processor with capers. Blend until fairly smooth.
4. Add salt and pepper and blend a few seconds.
5. Place pate in terrine or heavy, small serving bowl; cover and refrigerate for at least one hour or longer.
6. Brush bread with oil and toast in oven.
7. Spread toast with cold pate and serve.

Yield: 1-1/2 cups pate
Preparation: 25 minutes
Refrigeration: at least 1 hour

A good, simple pate for liver-lovers.

ROAST PORK LOIN

A LA - Cafe Juanita

1	**(3 lb.) pork loin** (de-boned)
	garlic (chopped) (lots of it depending on taste)
1/2	**cup olive oil**
1/2	**jar (4oz.) Grey Poupon Dijon mustard**
1/2	**t. rosemary**
	salt and pepper (to taste)
1	**cup cream**

1. Preheat oven to 350 degrees.
2. Mix together: one half the garlic; and all the oil, mustard, rosemary and salt and pepper.
3. In center cavity of meat, sprinkle the rest of the chopped garlic.
4. Then spread one half the mustard sauce all over. Roll roast and tie. Spread rest of mustard sauce over outside of roast. (If not enough, make more sauce).
5. Bake 1 hour and 20 minutes - longer if larger roast - but <u>do not</u> overcook pork.
6. Remove roast and de-grease drippings.
7. Add cream and reduce by cooking over medium-high heat for about 15 minutes. Sauce will become a rich, light caramel color.
8. Slice and pour sauce over and serve.

Serves: 4-6
Preparation: 30 minutes
Baking: 1 hour 20 minutes

So easy and so good! Yummy sauce!

BAKED PEARS

A LA - Cafe Juanita

6	**pears** (ripe, stems on, unpeeled)
18	**whole cloves**
1/2	**cup sugar**
1/2	**cup red wine**
	cream (garnish)
1/2	**t. ground cloves**

1. Preheat oven to 400º.
2. Stick 3 cloves in each pear.
3. Dissolve sugar in wine. Add 1/2 teaspoon ground cloves.
4. Place pears in baking dish and pour sugar/wine mixture over them.
5. Place in oven for 35-40 minutes until sauce is reduced to a syrup consistency. While pears are in oven, ladel sauce over them several times during the baking.
6. Remove from oven and cool pears. (If you like - they also taste delicious warm)
7. Pour syrup over them when serving. Then pour 1 tablespoon fresh cream over each.

Serves: 6
Preparation: 45 minutes

**Sauce is so good, you'll want to eat every last drop.
The colors are very festive. A delicious dessert on a cold
winter's night in front of a glowing fire.**

the Canal

Seattle is bisected by a canal and Lake Union, which connect Puget Sound and Lake Washington. How fitting to have The Canal Restaurant giving you a panoramic view of the canal and its veritable parade of ships!

Constructed in true Northwest style: solid cedar, vaulted ceiling and spacious decks, the Canal choices abound. Enjoy a gorgeous view and absorb the sunshine, original mural batiks and mosaics in a vaulted dining room. You can also visit the fireside lounge, where the sound of the crackling fire will smother out the tapping rain on a brisk Northwest evening.

Try their New York Pepper Steak - it's memorable. And once you've had their Canal Coffee, you'll order it over and over again - or make it at home. The recipes follow.

Serving lunch, dinner and Sunday brunch, the Canal offers ample parking and boat moorage.

The Canal is located at 5300 24th Avenue N.W., Seattle. Call 783-1964 for reservations.

ORIENTAL CHICKEN SESAME SALAD

A LA - The Canal

8	oz. boneless, skinless chicken breast meat
2	T. flour (seasoned with salt and pepper)
2	T. butter
1/2	t. sesame oil
1/4	cup oyster sauce*
1	cup water
1/4	cup soy sauce
1/2	cup sugar
1/4	t. sesame oil
1	T. wine vinegar
1	T. cornstarch (mixed with 1 T. water)
4	asparagus spears (lightly cooked)
12	pea pods (lightly cooked)
4	peeled carrots (thinly sliced on diagonal)
2	celery stalks (thinly sliced on diagonal)
1	small head bok choy (sliced lengthwise)
1/2	cup green onion (diced)
4	tomatoes (cut in wedges)
2	T. sesame seeds

1. Coat chicken in flour; dust off excess.
2. Heat butter and oil in fry pan over medium-low heat.
3. Saute chicken for approximately 10 minutes in pan until done and golden brown. Let cool and slice in julienne pieces (see Glossary for *julienne*).
4. Make sauce by combining oyster sauce, water, soy, sugar, sesame oil and vinegar in pan over high heat.
5. Bring to a boil; add cornstarch water mixture. Let cool.

- continued -

6. Assemble salad starting with vegetables layered in salad bowl.
7. Top with julienned chicken pieces.
8. Pour sauce over salad, garnish with green onions, sesame seeds and tomato wedges.

Serves: 4
Preparation: 20 minutes

*A brown thick bottled sauce available in the Oriental section of your local grocery store. Available at Safeway.

A delightful flavor combination. Great for lunch on a warm spring/summer day.

CANAL GREEK SALAD

A LA - The Canal

Vinaigrette Dressing
1/2   cup wine-vinegar
1   coddled egg*
8   anchovies (diced)
1/2   t. fresh or dried parsley
1/2   t. fresh or dried tarragon
1/2   t. fresh or dried oregano
1/2   t. salt and pepper
1   cup olive oil

Salad
2   cucumbers (peeled and diced)
3   tomatoes (diced)
1/2   red onion (julienned)
5   green onions (diced)
1/2   lb. feta cheese (cubed)
1/2   lb. Greek olives

Vinaigrette Dressing
1.   Combine wine-vinegar, egg, anchovies and seasonings in bowl or food processor.
2.   Whisk constantly while slowly adding oil until thickened slightly.
Salad
3.   In large bowl, combine cucumbers, tomatoes, onions, cheese and olives and dressing. Toss lightly.
4.   Serve immediately or refrigerate to chill.

Serves: 4-8
Preparation: 10 minutes

*To coddle egg, place egg in boiling water. Turn off heat and cover pan for 6 minutes.

A colorful combination of flavors. Perfect as a refreshing 1st course or as accompaniment to grilled meats.

44

NEW YORK PEPPER STEAK

A LA - The Canal

4	**strips bacon** (sliced in 2" pieces)
10	**mushrooms** (chopped)
5	**green onions** (sliced and julienned)*
4	**(8 oz.) New York steaks**
1/2	**cup crushed black peppercorns**
2	**shallots** (finely minced)
2/3	**cup Burgundy wine**
1/2	**cup whipping cream**
3	**T. butter**

1. Preheat oven to broil.
2. Saute bacon on stove until crisp. Add mushrooms and cook until tender. Next, add and saute green onions.
3. Remove ingredients and set aside.
4. Press pepper onto both sides of steaks. Broil until desired doneness, about 1-2 minutes each side for rare. Keep warm.

5. Combine shallots and burgundy in small sauce pan over high heat.
6. Reduce by half and add cream.
7. When cream is hot, but not boiling, remove from heat.
8. Quickly whisk in butter to a smooth, rich consistency.
9. To serve: cover plate with sauce; top with steak and garnish with sauteed bacon and mushrooms.

Serves: 4
Preparation: 10 minutes, depending on steak

*To julienne is to cut into long thin 1-1/2" strips.

**A N.W. version of a culinary classic.
Great!**

STRAWBERRIES GRAND MARNIER

A LA - The Canal

2	t. clarified butter
1	cup fresh strawberries (sliced)
1	T. sugar
1-1/2	T. Grand Marnier

1. Over very high heat, saute butter, berries and sugar until liquified, stirring constantly.
2. Add Grand Marnier and let alcohol burn off, all the while stirring. Cool.
3. Serve as topping for vanilla ice cream or cheese cake.

Serves:4
Preparation: 35 minutes

The perfect use for N.W. berries and so easy! Use your imagination for various other ways to use the recipe.

CANAL COFFEE

A LA - The Canal

1/2	oz. Metaxa liqueur
1/2	oz. Courvousier liqueur
1/2	oz. Tia Maria liqueur
1/2	cup black coffee
1	T. whipped cream

1. Combine 3 liqueurs in coffee cup or glass mug.
2. Add coffee and top with whipped cream.
3. Serve immediately!

Serves: 1
Preparation: 1-2 minutes

A perfect cool evening drink. Makes for mellow sipping.

Chez Shea

Enter the private, secret hide-away of Chez Shea. Hidden upstairs in a historical building in the heart of the Pike Place Market is a romantic setting with a view of Elliott Bay and the Market roof tops.

You'll feel as though Sandy Shea has welcomed you into her home with the rich wood foyer and antiques adding warmth and character to the coral-colored walls and unique art.

The real art, however, comes from the kitchen, with such wonders as: Roasted Tenderloin of Beef with Cognac Chanterelle Cream Sauce, and Warm Autumn Salad, with its surprising array of flavor combinations.

Everything comes together incredibly well here: the fresh food, the ambiance, and the view. The secret, of course, is Sandy's superb staff, and her insistance and reliance on the Market's daily fresh sheet, or produce announcement, which allows her to be both creative and flexible in offering some of the most delectable French cuisine with Northwest flair. Enjoy a four course dinner Prix Fixe, Tuesday through Sunday.

Chez Shea is located at 94 Pike St., Suite 34 in Seattle.
Call 467-9990 for reservations.

WARM AUTUMN SALAD

A LA - Chez Shea

1	**large bunch watercress**
1	**bunch arugula** (this small leafy green can be omitted or substituted with another green)
1	**T. fresh ginger** (peeled and diced)
2	**T. shallots** (diced)
1/4	**cup prosciutto**
2	**T. peanut oil**
1/2	**small head red cabbage** (thinly sliced)
3/4	**cup orange juice**
3	**T. balsamic vinegar** (readily available at local markets-but you may substitute red-wine vinegar if you wish)
1/3	**cup fennel bulb or fresh fennel** (chopped)
1/2	**cup green apple** (chopped)
6	**oz. smoked chicken breast** (thinly sliced)
12	**smoked oysters**
1	**T. orange rind** (grated)
1/4	**cup pine nuts** (optional)
	pomegranate seeds (optional)

1. Wash and trim watercress and arugula. Arrange on serving plate.
2. Saute ginger, shallots, and prosciutto in peanut oil for 1-2 minutes.
3. Add red cabbage, saute until just limp.
4. Add orange juice and vinegar. Simmer for 4 minutes.
5. Add fennel and apple; simmer 2-3 minutes. Season with salt and pepper to your taste.
6. Place cabbage mixture on top of greens.
7. Top with smoked chicken and oysters.
8. Garnish with orange rind, pine nuts and pomegranate seeds.

Serves: 4
Preparation: 15 minutes

A colorful combination with with an Oriental flavor.

50

ROASTED TENDERLOIN of BEEF with COGNAC CHANTERELLE CREAM SAUCE

A LA - Chez Shea

2-1/2-3 lbs.	beef tenderloin
2	T. peanut oil
3/4	cup cognac
3	shallots (finely chopped)
1	lb. chanterelles (sliced) or other wild mushroom
1-1/2	cups beef stock
1/2	cup heavy cream

1. Preheat oven 400º.
2. Brown all sides of tenderloin in peanut oil.
3. Transfer to oven-proof pan and bake to desired degree of doneness, 25-30 minutes for rare.
4. Remove from pan and let rest.
5. Deglaze* pan with cognac over high heat. Reduce liquid to half.
6. Add shallots, mushrooms and beef stock. Simmer 5 minutes.
7. Pour in cream; reduce to desired sauce consistency by cooking over medium heat.
8. Slice tenderloin; serve topped with sauce.

Serves: 4
Preparation: 45 minutes

*See Glossary for *Deglaze*.

A perfect use for chanterelles but delicious with any mushroom.

LEMON MOUSSE

A LA - Chez Shea

3	**egg yolks**
1/3	**cup granulated sugar**
1	**cup whipping cream**
3	**egg whites**
1/3	**cup sugar**
1/8	**cup white wine**
2	**t. unflavored gelatin**
1/3	**cup lemon juice** (freshly squeezed)
1-1/2	**t. grated lemon rind**
	fresh berries and mint (garnish)

1. In a mixing bowl, combine egg yolks and 1/3 cup sugar. Mix until thick. Transfer to large bowl.
2. Whip cream until thick and fold into egg yolk mixture.
3. Whip egg whites with remaining 1/3 cup sugar until stiff. Set aside.
4. In non-aluminum sauce pan, combine wine, gelatin, lemon juice and rind.
5. Heat over low heat just until gelatin dissolves.
6. Using a wire whisk add gelatin mixture to egg yolk cream mixture.
7. Fold in egg whites and chill.
8. Ladle into wine glasses; garnish with berries and mint.

Serves: 4
Preparation: 25 minutes

A wonderful light dessert. Perfect accompaniment to strawberries or raspberries or alone.

BAY HOUSE

MARKET PLACE

Cutter's Bayhouse, according to Colman Andrews, food critic for Metropolitan Home magazine is "one of the ten best Amercian Bistro's".

Cutter's is located at Seattle's colorful Pike Place Market. The bistro is big, bright and noisy with modern accents of peach and grey. An expansive view captures Mount Rainier, the city skyline, busy Elliott Bay and colorful sunsets behind the Olympic Mountains.

At Cutter's, both the menu and the hours are long. Like the clientele, the menu is stylish, eclectic, international— and constantly changing. Selections like: Yaki Soba, Cajun Fettucine with Chicken, Kal Bi Ribs, Ahi Carpaccio, Mesquite Grilled Lamb with Fresh Rosemary Crust, Alaska Sea Scallops with Port-Citrus Sauce, Copper River King Salmon with Toasted Hazlenut Butter and Pear Bread Pudding with Bourbon Sauce are all served from an energetic display kitchen. The Homemade Focaccia, Italian Pan Bread with Fresh Garlic and Rosemary, is baked fresh throughout the day.

To take the pulse of Seattle's night life, come and enjoy Cutter's, Seattle's go anytime, order anything restaurant.

Cutter's Bayhouse is located at 2001 Western Avenue, Seattle. Call 448-4884 for reservations.

BAKED CHICKEN DIJON
(start in a.m. or night before to marinate)

A LA - Cutters Bay House

4   **boneless, skinless chicken breasts**

Marinade
1   **cube butter**
1   **clove garlic** (mashed)
5   **t. Dijon mustard**

Breading
2   **T. fresh parsley** (minced)
5   **T. Parmesan cheese** (shedded)
1-1/2 **cups Panko bread crumbs** (these are delicious Japanese bread crumbs found in most grocery stores)

Garnish
Dijon mustard
mayonnaise
parmesan cheese (finely shredded)

Marinade
1.   Melt butter in saute pan over low heat.
2.   Add garlic and simmer for 5 minutes on low.
3.   Blend in mustard, stirring well.
4.   Remove from heat and let cool enough to touch but not solidify. Discard garlic. Whip vigorously until mixture thickens. Set aside.

- continued -

Breading

5. Mix parsley, cheese and bread crumbs together, blending well.

6. Dip chicken in butter mixture, coating all surfaces, then in breading mixture, packing crumbs onto chicken to coat well.

7. Place chicken in single layer in low pan. Cover and refrigerate for several hours to set breading.

8. Bake at 350° for 12 minutes. Chicken should be lightly browned and moist on inside.

Garnish

9. Mix equal parts of Dijon and mayonnaise together and serve as a topping on the side. Top each breast with parmesan cheese and serve.

Serves: 4
Preparation: 30 minutes
Refrigeration: at least 3 to 4 hours
Baking: 12 minutes

Yummy, moist and easy. The bread crumbs and buttery Dijon make a delicious combination.

BLUM'S COFFEE TOFFEE PIE

A LA - Cutters Bay House

Pastry Shell
5   oz. **pie crust mix**
1-3/4 oz. **brown sugar**
3   oz. **walnuts** (finely chopped)
1   oz. **bittersweet chocolate** (grated) (Guittard brand recommended)
1   **T. water**
1   **t. vanilla**

Coffee Topping
2   **cups whipping cream**
2   **T. instant coffee granules**
2-1/4 oz. **confectioners sugar**

Filling
4   oz. (1/2 cup) **butter** (softened)
5-1/2 oz. **granulated sugar**
2   **t. instant coffee granules**
2   **large eggs**
1   oz. **bittersweet chocolate** (melted and cooled)

Garnish
1   oz. **semi-sweet chocolate** (grated) (Guittard recommended)

Pastry Shell
1. Combine pie crust mix with brown sugar, walnuts and chocolate. Add water and vanilla. Mix well with a fork until crumbly and slightly moist in texture.
2. Transfer pie crust mix to well greased 9" pie plate. Firmly press mix against sides and bottom.
3. Bake in 350º oven for 10 minutes. Cool.

- continued -

Coffee Topping
4. Mix all ingredients together; cover and refrigerate for 1 hour to allow granules to dissolve.

Filling
5. Using electric mixer (do not use processor), beat butter until white and creamy, about 3 minutes.
6. Gradually add granulated sugar and coffee and beat about 4 minutes. Scrape bowl.
7. Add one egg; beat 10 minutes. Add remaining egg; beat 10 minutes or until filling is a pudding-like consistency. Add chocolate and beat.
8. Spoon filling into cooled pie shell and refrigerate at least 6 hours or overnight.
9. When ready to serve, remove cream from refrigerator and beat until stiff peaks form.
10. Spoon topping onto pie.

Garnish
11. Garnish with grated semi-sweet chocolate and serve.

Yield: 1 (9") pie
Preparation: 1 hour
Refrigeration: at least 6 hours or overnight

from the publisher:
To illustrate how good this pie actually is (it's sheer delight), I planned to include it years before the book was actually published. You won't be disappointed - just beat those eggs a long time and reap the rewards.

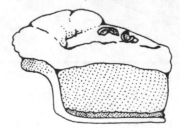

Daniel's Broiler

Daniel's is a beautiful restaurant. Once inside you'll see why it has become the talk of the town. Small and cozy, Daniel's overlooks moored sailboats on Lake Washington.

With a welcoming entrance, onyx tables, a huge copper chandelier and multi-beamed ceiling, Daniel's has a sophisticated and plush atmosphere.

Paralleling the atmosphere in quality is the food: aged steaks, fresh seafood, delicious salads such as their own *Caesar Salad*, and tempting desserts, such as the mouthwatering *Mocha Fudge Pie* (which recipe follows), will delight you. Summer deck seating will lure you; valet parking will pamper you and boat slips will accomodate your yacht.

Daniel's Broiler is located at 200 Lake Washington Blvd., Seattle. Call 329-4191 for reservations .

CAESAR SALAD

A LA - Daniel's Broiler

1	**head romaine lettuce**
1	**egg** (coddled-see step 2)
1/4	**cup salad oil**
2	**T. anchovie fillets** (minced)
2	**t. fresh garlic** (minced)
2	**T. red wine vinegar**
1/4	**t. Worchestershire sauce**
1/2	**t. dry mustard powder**
1/4	**t. freshly ground black pepper**
1	**t. lemon juice**
	croutons (as desired)
1/3	**cup parmesan** (grated)
1/4	**cup parmesan** (shredded)

1. Trim all dark or wilted parts from the romaine. Wash whole head well in 85º water. Trim 1/4 off top of head and stand head up in refrigerator for 8-12 hours before use.
2. To coddle egg, place in dish, pour boiling water over and let stand till room temperature (this takes 30-40 minutes).
3. Combine coddled egg, oil and mix well in salad bowl.
4. Add anchovie, garlic, vinegar, Worchestershire, mustard, pepper and lemon. Mix well.
5. Add romaine, cut into 1 inch square pieces, croutons and grated parmesan. Toss well.
6. Serve on chilled plates and top with shredded parmesan.

Serves:4
Preparation: 15 minutes
Refrigeration: 8-12 hours for romaine
Coddle egg: 30-40 minutes

A classic Caesar - add tomatoes if you desire.

FETTUCCINE SEASIDE

A LA - Daniel's Broiler

2	**cups fettuccine** (pre-cooked, al dente*)
1/2	**cup butter** (clarified*)
1/2	**t. fresh garlic** (minced)
1/2	**cup fresh salmon** (cut in 1/2" cubes)
1/2	**cup scallops**
1	**cup fresh mushrooms** (sliced)
1/2	**t. seasoning salt**
1	**cup whipping cream**
1/2	**cup sour cream**
2	**T. Parmesan cheese** (shredded)
2	**T. Romano cheese** (shredded)
1/2	**cup bay shrimp**
1/2	**cup spinach** (fresh, thinly shredded)
	lemon wedges and parsley sprigs (garnish)

1. Have fettuccine cooked al dente and set aside.
2. In frying pan heat butter over medium heat; add garlic, salmon, scallops and mushrooms.
3. Season all ingredients evenly with half the seasoning salt. Cook until seafoods are half done, about 2 minutes.
4. Add pasta; season evenly with remaining seasoning salt and blend well.
5. Mix whipping cream, sour cream and both cheeses into pasta., Mix well.
6. Cook 3-5 minutes over medium heat, stirring frequently until creamy.
7. Add shrimp and spinach; mix well; cook until warm and serve on plate with lemon and parsley garnish.

Serves: 4
Preparation: 20 minutes total

*See Glossary for clarified or *al dente*.

Easy and good!

MOCHA FUDGE PIE
(refrigerate overnight or 9 hours)

A LA - Daniel's Broiler

1/2	of 8oz. pkg. **Nabisco Famous Chocolate Wafers**
1/4	**cup butter** (melted)
1	**qt. Dreyer's Grand Coffee Ice Cream**
1-1/2	**cups fudge topping** (softened or slightly heated)
	whipped cream (garnish)
	chopped walnuts (garnish)
	chocolate shavings (garnish)

1. Crush or grind wafers into medium fine crumbs.
2. In bowl, combine wafer crumbs and butter. Mix well.
3. Press crumbs and butter mixture into 9" pie dish to form crust.
4. Fill pie crust with softened coffee ice cream. Put pie in freezer until hard.
5. When pie is frozen hard, spread with fudge topping. Return to freezer for 8 hours.
6. To serve: cut into 8 pieces. Place each piece on chilled plate and top with sweetened whipped cream, walnuts and chocolate shavings.

Serves: 1 (9") pie or 8 servings
Preparation: 15 minutes
Freezing: 9 hours (1 hour plus 8 hours)

Absolutely delicious and so <u>EASY</u>. Another great party dessert you can prepare ahead.

62

If you're partial to Northwest sunsets, fishing piers and sandy beaches, you'll enjoy The Lobster Shop, featured by PM Magazine as "that quaint hide-a-way to bring out of town guests".

Within the character of a weathered beach house, you'll savor the lobster, king crab and clam chowder in this cozy spot, steps from the water.

There is both an intimate upstairs room and cozy downstairs, seating loyal patrons from far and near who come for the best lobster on the West Coast. Australian Rock Lobster Tails, Hood Canal Clams and Hama Hama Oysters are outstanding as well as the Gulf Prawns and Alaskan King Crab Legs.

The Lobster Shop now has two locations to serve you; the original Dash Point Beach location and the modern, multi-level construction at Ruston Way which epitomizes Northwest design with its decks, large glass walls and formidable views of Commencement Bay.

Either location is certain to provide a truly memorable dining experience.

The Dash Point Lobster Shop is located at 6912 Soundview Dr. N.E., Tacoma. Call 1-800-232-7478 for reservations. There is a second location at 4013 Ruston Way, 759-2165.

HOUSE DRESSING

A LA - The Dash Point Lobster Shop

1	cup red wine vinegar
1/2	cup cider vinegar
1/2	cup white vinegar
1/2	cup water
1	T. pepper (coarse ground)
1	T. salt
1	T. whole thyme
1	T. whole tarragon
2/3	T. dry mustard
1-1/3	cups parmesan cheese (grated)
1-1/3	T. granulated sugar
2-1/3	cups salad oil

1. Combine all ingredients in blender or food processor.
2. Mix thoroughly and refrigerate to allow flavors to combine.
3. Serve over favorite mixed greens.

Yield: 1 quart
Preparation: 5 minutes
Refrigeration: several hours for all flavors to blend.

Chef recommends a salad with torn lettuce, cherry tomatoes, green onion, cucumber, sunflower seeds and crumbled bleu cheese to accompany dressing.

A popular choice!

MUSSEL APPETIZER

A - LA - The Dash Point Lobster Shop

1/3	**cup red wine vinegar**
1/2	**cup red wine**
1/2	**cup** (melted) **butter**
2	**t. ground thyme**
2	**t. garlic** (minced)
1/2	**cup water**
1-1/2	**to 2 lbs. mussels** (preferably 2" long and tightly closed) scrubbed and debearded.

1. Combine vinegar, wine, butter, thyme, garlic and water in large pot and bring to rolling boil.
2. Place mussels in steaming rack and lower into large pot.
3. Steam mussels until they've just opened. Do not overcook.
4. Serve mussels in large bowl with 1/3 cup broth spooned over them.

Serves: 2-4 appetizers
Preparation: 10 minutes

A different version of steamed mussels. Try and enjoy!

DASH POINT CIOPPINO AND PORTUGUESE LOBSTER POT

A LA - Dash Point Lobster Shop

Cioppino Base

1-1/4	**cups onion** (chopped coarsely)
3	**carrots** (chopped coarsely)
3	**cups canned tomatoes** (diced-with the puree)
3	**cups tomato sauce**
1/2	**cup green chilies** (chopped)
1	**t. garlic** (chopped)
1/2	**cup red wine**
1-1/2	**T. whole thyme**
3/4	**t. rosemary**
2	**T. fresh basil** or 1 T. dry
	salt and pepper (to taste)
1-1/2	**cups water**
1/2	**lb. each salmon, halibut; King Crab** (in shell) **and shrimp** (in shell)
8	**medium prawns**
32	**each clams and mussels in shell**
4	(5 oz.) **lobster tails, split in half** (optional*)
	lemon (garnish)

1. In large stock pot: steam onion and carrots until just tender.
2. Add tomatoes, tomato sauce, chilies, garlic and red wine. Heat to simmer.
3. Add thyme, rosemary, basil, salt and pepper and water. Heat again to simmer.
4. Base can be refrigerated or frozen at this point.

- continued -

5.   To serve, heat 40 ounces of cioppino base to simmering.
6.   Add remaining ingredients and cook until fish and
prawns are opaque and clams and mussels have
opened.
7.   Serve immediately garnished with lemon.

Serves: 4
Proparation: 1 1/2 hours

*Use lobster in lobster pot only- not in cioppino.

**A favorite of patrons. Try with and without lobster tail for
a special meal.**

AUSTRALIAN ROCK LOBSTER TAIL

A LA - The Dash Point Lobster Shop

4	(8 oz.) **Australian Rock Lobster Tails.** Can be larger if appetites and budgets permit.
1	**lb. butter** (melted)
1	**t. Spanish or regular paprika** (optional)
2	**lemons** (cut in wedges)

1. Thaw lobster tails in cold water, approximately 1 hour.
2. Using sharp knife or scissors cut shell down the back.
3. Remove tail meat carefully from shells but do not detach from base of shells.
4. Cut meat from head to tail half way through to remove dark veins. Discard veins.
5. Preheat oven to 425º.
6. Place tails in baking dish large enough to hold 4 tails. Fan tails and meat slightly.
7. Fill pan with 3/4" warm water.
8. Brush tails thoroughly with melted butter. Sprinkle with paprika for color.
9. Place pan in oven. Bake until meat becomes whitish and opaque, a few minutes each side but time depends on size. <u>DO NOT OVER COOK as meat will be tough and rubbery!</u>
10. Serve warm with lots of melted butter and garnished with lemon wedges.

Serves:4
Preparation: 15 minutes

An elegant meal - done to perfection.

The Lobster Shop notes that they use only Australian Rock lobsters because their fresh quality and sweet taste surpasses any warm water tails (Hawaiian, Brazilian, Floridian, etc.).

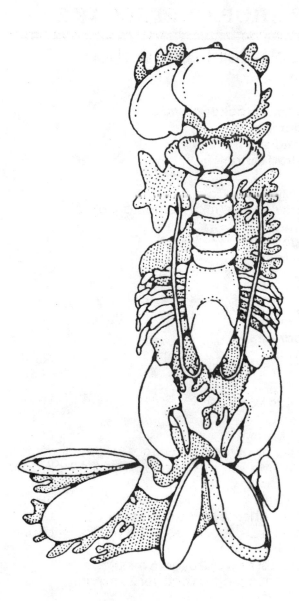

LOBSTER SHOP CHEESECAKE

A LA - The Dash Point Lobster Shop

Crust
1	**cup graham cracker crumbs**
1/4	**cup sugar**
1	**t. cinnamon**
1/4	**cup melted butter**

Cheescake
3/4	**lb. cream cheese** (room temperature)
1/2	**cup sugar**
2	**large eggs**
1/4	**lemon** (juiced)
1/2	**T. vanilla**

Topping
12	**oz. sour cream**
1/4	**cup sugar**
1/2	**T. vanilla**

1. Preheat oven 350º.

Crust
2. Make crust by combining crumbs, sugar, cinnamon and butter. Mix until well blended. Pat into 9" pie pan.

Cheesecake
3. Beat cream cheese until soft and runny.
4. Add sugar, eggs, lemon juice and vanilla. Beat until blended.
5. Pour into crust and bake for 25 minutes.
6. Remove from oven and cool for 25 minutes.

- continued -

Topping

7. Blend sour cream, sugar and vanilla. Let stand for 5-10 minutes so sugar dissolves.
8. Spread on cooled cheesecake. Return to oven for additional 10 minutes.
9. Remove pie and let cool 30-45 minutes then refrigerate covered with saran wrap, until well chilled (several hours or overnight).

Serves: 6
Preparation: 1 hour
Refrigeration: several hours at least (best overnight).

Best if made 1 day ahead. An easy, tasty version of an all time favorite.

71

JUMBO GULF STREAM PRAWNS

A LA - The Dash Point Lobster Shop

2	**lbs. jumbo prawns** (peeled and deveined, tails on)
1	**lb. unsalted clarified* butter**
4-8	**garlic cloves, depending on taste** (chopped)
1	**lemon** (cut in wedges)

1. Preheat oven to 400º.
2. In baking pan, combine butter, chopped garlic cloves and juice from one lemon. Let set to combine flavors.
3. Arrange prawns on top of butter mixture, leaving 1/4" space between prawns.
4. Bake in oven 2-3 minutes until just pink.
5. Turn prawns over and bake for 3 more minutes or until cooked, Do not overcook.
6. Remove prawns from pan. Let excess butter drain before arranging on plate.
7. Serve with remaining garlic butter and lemon wedges.

Serves: 4
Preparation: 10 minutes

*See Glossary for *clarified*.

In 10 minutes you can have a delicious meal on the table for family or guests.

72

B A R & G R I L L

Whether you've just come from a Sonics game or the symphony, you'll find Duke's Bar and Grill to be more than just a neighborhood bistro.

"Fresh" and "fresh daily" are words that pop up all over the menu at Duke's. This, in addition to its location five blocks north of the Seattle Center, is what draws sports celebrities, as well as theater and symphony buffs.

Seattle's own Duke Moscrip, who started Duke's after having owned Ray's Boathouse, was one of the first to serve very good wines and champagne by the glass and feature "fragmented dining for the slim set", which means smaller portions of anything on the menu. The Rack of Lamb is tender perfection and we can't say enough about the Praline Cheesecake; try them (the recipes follow). If a Seattle downpour catches you sneezing, come in for some of the best chicken soup in the West, to rival any Jewish Grandmother's. Have lunch until 3:00 or dine until midnight. The fresh home-cooking, antique bar and blue and white checked linen will remind you of days bone by, when service and good food were inseparable.

Duke's has two distinct locations to serve you:
10116 NE 8th, Bellevue. Call 455-5775;
and 236 1st West, Seattle. Call 283-4400.

TEMPURA BATTER

A LA - Duke's Bar & Grill

3/4	**cup cornstarch**
3/4	**cup rice flour**
1/2	**t. baking powder**
	pinch of salt
1	**medium egg** (beaten)
1/4	**cup ice cubes**
3/4	**cup club soda**
	assorted fresh vegetables (to serve 4)

           zucchini (sliced)
           eggplant (diced)
           sweet potatoes (sliced)
           mushrooms (whole)
           onion rings

1/2-1	**cup cornstarch**
2-3	**cups vegetable oil**

1. Combine cornstarch, rice flour, baking powder and salt.
2. Add egg and mix.
3. Add ice and soda and mix for 1 minute (mixture will not blend).
4. Dust vegetables with cornstarch and dip in batter.
5. Cook in hot oil (375°) until batter is a golden color. Serve immediately.

Serves: 4 as appetizer
Preparation: 15 minutes

Try batter with prawns, chicken or white fish. It's fun and easy!

SPICY SZECHUAN CHICKEN WITH HOT AND SOUR SAUCE

A LA - Duke's Bar & Grill

1	cup flour
1	cup cornstarch
1/2	t. white pepper
1/4	t. salt
1	t. baking powder
1/4	t. baking soda
2	T. beer
1	t. salad oil
1	lb. boneless, skinless chicken breast (cut in 1/2" strips)
1-2	cups oil for frying

Sauce

2	cups red wine vinegar
1	cup brown sugar
1	cup granulated sugar
1	cup pineapple juice
1/2	cup water
1/2	T. red pepper sauce (Durkee Hot Sauce recommended)
1	t. crushed red pepper
1	t. red curry paste*
1/2	T. tamarind paste (optional)
1/4	cup grenadine syrup*
1/2	T. ginger root (minced)
1/4	cup cornstarch mixed with 1/4 cup water

1. Combine flour, cornstarch, pepper, salt, baking powder and soda.
2. Add beer and oil. Stir to mix. Batter should be thick enough to coat chicken. If too thick, thin with additional beer.

- continued -

76

3.   Coat chicken pieces well.
4.   Heat oil to hot. Drop pieces in and cook for about 2
        minutes until golden

        Sauce.
5.   In sauce pan combine all sauce ingredients except
        cornstarch and bring to boil.
6.   Combine cornstarch with one quarter cup water. Stir.
7.   Add to sauce; cook until thickened.
8.   Sauce will keep 2-3 weeks refrigerated.

Serves: 2 as entree; 4 as appetizer
Preparation: 25 minutes

*Find in Oriental food store.
**Grenadine is a drink mixer you'll find in beverage section of
supermarket.

**The test kitchen re-tested this one many times over-why?
Because it's so delicious!**

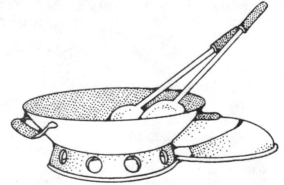

PRALINE CHEESECAKE

A LA - Duke's Bar & Grill

Graham cracker crust (unbaked)

1-1/3	**cups graham cracker crumbs**
1/3	**cup brown sugar**
1/2	**t. cinnamon** (optional)
1/3	**cup melted butter**

Filling

3	**lbs. cream cheese** (softened)
1/4	**cup flour** (sifted)
1	**cup granulated sugar**
2	**cups brown sugar**
1	**t. lemon juice**
1/4	**t. vanilla**
3	**eggs**
8	**oz. toasted chopped almonds**

Crust

1. Combine graham cracker crumbs, brown sugar, cinnamon and melted butter. Blend. Press into 10" spring form pan. Refrigerate.

Filling

2. Put room temperature cream cheese in food processor a little at a time until blended and smooth. Add flour and blend.
3. Gradually add sugars until blended.
4. Add lemon ,vanilla, eggs (one at a time); process until blended. Fold in almonds.
5. Pour or spoon filling into crust-lined spring form pan.

- continued -

6.   Bake at 200° for 1-1/2 to 2 hours or until done. Cake will rise slightly and sink when taken out of oven. (If oven bakes hot, put a pan with a pint of water in the oven under the rack with the cake)
7.   Let cool and refrigerate overnight.

Serves: 10-12
Preparation: 30 minutes
Baking: 1-1/2 to 2 hours

A great variation of our all-time favorite! Very rich!

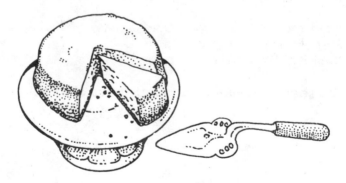

FAMOUS RACK OF LAMB MARINADE
(Marinate Lamb at least 48 hours ahead)

A LA - Duke's Bar & Grill

1-1/2	**cups apple juice**
1	**cup soy sauce**
1	**T. lemon juice**
1/2	**T. garlic** (finely chopped)
1	**large orange** (juice only)
1-2	**racks of lamb** (prime New Zealand lamb recommended)

1. Combine all ingredients except lamb, and bring to a boil.
2. Remove from heat; cool.
3. Completely immerse racks in marinade.
4. Marinate in refrigerator at least 48 hours.
5. Drain racks and cook as desired, grilled or baked.
6. Marinade can be re-used 2 more times when kept under refrigeration.
7. If it becomes cloudy, discard.

Yield: marinates 2 racks (about 3 cups)
Preparation: 5 minutes
Marinate Time: at least 48 hours

The secret to Duke's wonderful racks of lamb!

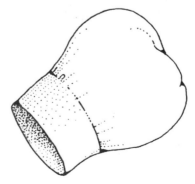

80

The Famous PACIFIC DESSERT Company

The Famous Pacific Dessert Company has already earned its name from such wonders as Chocolate Decadence, Sinful Chocolate and Amaretto Cheesecake.

What many don't know is that some of the fluffiest quiche, heartiest stew and freshest salad comes out of the very same kitchen.

After eating a wonderfully light salad sampler of Asparagus Walnut Salad, Primavera Pasta Salad and Fresh Fruit Salad, you can easily justify a rich cream-filled Zucotto Fiorentino or Dacquoise with its hazelnut and cream center. There is Breakfast Quiche, Frittata and Eggs an Cocotte, along with an Espresso happy hour from 8:30 to 10:30 and the aroma of fresh baked pastries wafting through the air of this Bellevue find.

Have a hot bowl of soup with a sandwich, salad and dessert, or daily specials like the Smoked Turkey and Wild Rice Salad (the recipe follows) until 9:00 p.m.

The Famous Pacific Dessert Company knows how to please its patrons, and if you've stayed away lest you be tempted by a rich dessert, never fear. They have an array of delicious, light specialties, such as Lemon Raspberry Mousse, Poached Pear in Blueberry Sauce or Fresh Strawberry Cake (a wedding cake favorite).

- continued -

The Famous Pacific Dessert Company sells wholesale cakes to restaurants from Edmonds to Tacoma, and has a national market with its Linzer Torte and Chocolate Decadence.

To treat yourself or someone else, the two of you or a large party, The Famous Pacific Dessert Company can fulfill your wishes. All of the Seattle stores have desserts, tortes, espresso and homemade ice cream, but lunch is served only at the Bellevue location.

The Famous Pacific Dessert Company is located just across from Bellevue Square at 10116 N.E. 8th, Bellevue.
Seattle locations: 2407 10th Avenue East, 127 Mercer Street, and 420 East Denny.

APRICOT GINGER SOUP

A LA - The Famous Pacific Dessert Co.

3   **lbs. fresh apricots** (very ripe)
1   **T. fresh ginger** (chopped)
1   **cup heavy cream**
1   **T. rum**

1.   Wash, and cut the apricots in half.
2.   Together with ginger, put through blender or processor until pureed. Strain.
3.   Add cream and rum and blend with whisk.
4.   Ladel into bowls and enjoy!

Yield: 6 cups (6-8 servings)
Preparation: 10 minutes

A perfect opener or finish to an elegant summer meal. So easy!

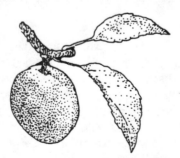

SMOKED TURKEY AND WILD RICE SALAD

A LA - The Famous Pacific Dessert Co.

3-3/4	**cups chicken stock**
6	**oz. wild rice**
2	**Bouquet Garnis** (make your own: Tie-up in 2 small cheese cloth pouches: parsley stems, bay leaves and thyme)
1	**onion** (chopped)
1	**T. butter**
6	**oz. white rice**
3/4	**t. salt**

	Vinaigrette dressing
6	**T. white wine vinegar**
2	**t. dijon mustard**
1	**cup walnut oil**
1-1/2	**T. dry tarragon**
	salt and pepper (to taste)

8	**oz. smoked turkey breast** (diced) Seattle Super Smoked brand is best)
1	**small bunch broccoli flowerettes** (blanched*)
1	**stalk celery** (sliced on a double bias)

1. Bring 2-1/4 cups stock to boil. Add wild rice and 1 Bouquet Garni. Cover and cook on low for 45-60 minutes, until done. Remove Bouquet. Fluff and cool.
2. Meanwhile, saute onion in butter; add white rice and mix. Add remaining 1-1/2 cups boiling stock, 1 Bouquet Garni and salt.
3. Cover and cook on low for 18 minutes. Remove Bouquet. Fluff and cool.

- continued -

84

Vinaigrette Dressing
4.   Mix 1 tablespoon vinegar with mustard. Slowly drizzle in oil while whisking vigorously. Then add remaining vinegar and tarragon and season with salt and pepper. Set aside.

5.   Toss rice, turkey, broccoli, celery and dressing, together. Chill at least 2 hours**.
6.   Soason to tacto boforo corving.

Serves: 6-8
Preparation: 1 hour
Refrigeration: at least 2 hours

*To blanch broccoli flowerettes, immerse them in boiling water for 3 minutes; then in cold water to stop cooking.
**If making salad day before, leave out broccoli and add following day as it discolors.

An interesting combination. Makes a great picnic dish.

RUM CUSTARD

A LA - Famous Pacific Dessert Co.

2	**cups sugar**
3/4	**cup water**
2	**cups half and half**
1/2	**cup sugar**
6	**egg yolks**
3	**T. dark rum**

1. Preheat oven 350°.
2. Combine sugar and water in sauce pan.
3. Over medium high heat bring mixture to a boil.
4. Boil until medium caramel colored. Using wet pastry brush, brush sides of pan so that crystals don't form. Do not let mixture burn.
5. Pour into 6 (4 oz.) ramekins or custard cups.
6. Mix half and half and sugar. Scald over medium heat and cool.
7. Whip egg yolks until lemon-colored. Stir into cooled cream.
8. Add rum; stir well.
9. Pour into ramekins over caramel.
10. Cover with foil. Place in shallow baking pan filled with hot water halfway up sides.
11. Bake for 30 minutes or until centers are firm.
12. Cool and refrigerate.
13. When ready to serve, run knife around edge of custard.
14. Set dishes in warm water for 1 minute.
15. Invert onto serving plates. Serve immediately.

Serves: 6
Preparation: 60 minutes

A nice variation of a classic and a favorite.

POACHED PEARS WITH BLUEBERRY SAUCE

A LA - Famous Pacific Dessert Co.

3	**pears** (Bartlett or Comice)
1/2	**lemon**
4	**cups white wine**
1/4	**cup sugar**
2	**cups blueberries** (fresh or frozen - pureed)
6	**mint leaves**

1. Peel, core and halve the pears. Set in water with juice from lemon. This prevents pears from turning brown.
2. Combine wine and sugar in sauce pan. Bring to a boil.
3. Drain pears; add to wine mixture.
4. Poach pears, at a simmer, until centers are almost soft, approximately 20 minutes. Pears should still feel firm.
5. Remove pears from liquid. Add blueberry puree to wine.
6. Reduce, over high heat, to one cup. Stir continually to prevent burning.
7. Place blueberry sauce on plate. Place pear on top.
8. Garnish with mint leaves.

Serves: 6
Preparation: 30 minutes

This dessert only has 85 calories so it is a perfect light dessert!

franco's
HIDDEN
HARBOR

Franco's Hidden Harbor is one of the oldest restaurants in Seattle. The original owner, John Franco, was the sole proprietor for 39 years, prior to selling to the present owners in 1985. The restaurant built its reputation on using fresh Northwest ingredients whenever possible and became especially well known for its specialty crab recipes. Present owners follow this long tradition, using only fresh ingredients for their daily specials.

Located on Westlake Avenue North, the restaurant has a relaxed, comfortable, unpretentious air about it. It is almost like entering a private club as you descend the stairs, leaving the bustle and cares of the everyday world ouside. Once seated, dining patrons can look out the wide expanse of glass to view an impressive array of cruisers.

Chef-partner Robin Day brings a long history in the Seattle restaurant business to this venture. His food and management expertise, as well as attention to detail, make dining at Franco's truly an event. Chef Day has chosen to share three of his personal favorites. Try the Baked Deviled Crab Oysters for an outstanding appetizer - or maybe make an entire meal of them!

Franco's Hidden Harbor is located at 1500 Westlake Avenue North, Seattle. Call 282-0501 for reservations.

89

BAKED DEVILED FRESH OYSTERS

A LA - Franco's Hidden Harbor

12	**fresh oysters on half shell** **rocksalt**
2	**eggs** (separated)
2	**cups cream sauce*** (Bechamel)
1/2	**lb. dungeness crabmeat**
2	**t. dry mustard**
2	**T. dry sherry**
1/16	**t. cayenne pepper** (pinch)
1/3	**cup parmesan cheese** (grated)

1. Preheat oven to broil.
2. Place oysters on bed of rock salt, in baking dish.
3. Beat egg whites until stiff; set aside.
4. Combine egg yolks, cream sauce, crabmeat, mustard, sherry and cayenne in sauce pan.
5. Over low heat, warm to lukewarm temperature.
6. Gently fold egg whites into crab mixture.
7. Spoon crab mixture over top of each oyster.
8. Top with parmesan cheese. Broil under broiler for 3 minutes until sauce is golden brown and oysters are hot.
9. Serve immediately.

Serves: 4 as appetizer; 2 as first course
Preparation: 15 minutes

*Buy packaged Bechamel Sauce in grocery store or make your own: Melt 4 tablespoons butter in pan and add 4 tablespoons flour. Stir constantly but do not brown (about 4-5 minutes). Add 2 cups boiling milk. Bring to boil again all the while stirring with a whisk. Cook for 5 minutes on medium heat. Season to taste with salt, pepper and nutmeg.

A must for oyster lovers. A great variation on a classic recipe.

90

FRANCO'S COMBINATION STEAMER BUCKET

A LA - Franco's Hidden Harbor

1	**lb. fresh pink scallops in shells**
1	**lb. fresh mussels** (beards removed)
1	**lb. fresh steamer clams**
1/2	**lb. butter**
4	**cups white wine** such as chablis, chardonnay, fume blanc
2	**cups water**
4	**t. garlic** (minced)
1/2	**t. crushed red chilis** (or to taste)
2	**cups fresh tomatoes** (diced)
8	**whole green onions** (root end removed)
2	**t. salt**
4	**t. fresh parsley** (chopped)

1. Rinse sand from shells of scallops, mussels and clams.
2. Place shellfish in sauce pan with tight lid.
3. Add all remaining ingredients.
4. Bring to a boil, place lid on pan; steam for 1 minute.
5. To serve, ladle shellfish into serving bowl, using vegetables as a garnish. Pour stock into mugs and serve as accompaniment*.

Serves: 4 as meal, 6-8 as 1st course
Preparation: 15 minutes

*If you prefer you can leave broth in bowl with seafood. But drinking the broth from a mug is one of "lifes little pleasures".

A great variation of a Northwest classic. Serve anytime for a casual meal that will be a hit.

ACAPULCO COCKTAIL

A LA - Franco's Hidden Harbor

1-1/2	**oz. amber rum**
3/4	**oz. triple sec** or Cointreau liqueur
1	**t. oregat syrup** (purchase in liquor store or grocery store)
1/3	**cup frozen lemonade concentrate**
1	**cup crushed ice**
	salt
	lime wheel

1. Place rum, triple sec, oregat, lemonade and ice in blender.
2. Blend on medium speed until a smooth slush.
3. Run lime around rim of 12 oz. wine glass. Dip rim in salt.
4. Pour slush into glass and garnish with lime wheel and serve.

Serves: 1
Preparation: 3 minutes

Cheers! A refreshing drink for a summer day or Mexican meal.

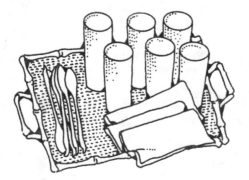

FULLERS

It used to be that a hotel was where you stayed or waited until you found a good restaurant. This of course, has changed, and is never more evident than with Fullers at the Sheraton, which serves lunch and dinner.

This fancy restaurant, located in an elegant hotel, offers a taste of the best of the Northwest. Not only is some famous Northwest art to be seen adorning the dining room, but what comes to your table is sheer art in presentation and quality. There is the Spicy Squash Bisque and Fresh Salmon Patties with Sweet Peppers and Lemon Herb Beurre Blanc, Halibut with Ginger Lime Butter and delicious pates and unforgettable desserts.

Desserts are a real specialty here. Anything you choose will be outstanding. If your insatiable sweet tooth twinges, there is a 27 foot long dessert spread in BANNERS to fill your every wish. Add to this a beautiful piano lounge featuring some terrific entertainment, and you have a highly acclaimed hotel restaurant.

Fullers is located at Sixth and Pike (Sheraton Hotel). Call 447-5544 for reservations.

SPICY SQUASH BISQUE

(Make Creme Fraiche, *optional*, night before)

A LA - Fullers

3	**T. butter**
2-1/2	**cups winter squash** (peeled and cubed) such as Hubbard, Acorn, Pumpkin etc.
1	**small onion** (finely diced)
2	**shallot onions** (finely diced)
1	**t. ground cardamon spice**
	pinch of cinnamon
1/4	**t. nutmeg**
	pinch of cumin
1/4	**t. ground coriander**
1/2-1	**cup pumpkin puree**
3	**cups good and rich chicken stock**
1/2	**t. salt** (to taste)
1	**carrot** (1" julienne cut)*
1	**leek, white part only** (1" julienne cut)*
1	**cup celery** (finely diced)
1	**cup canned corn**
3	**T. butter**
1-2	**cups cream** (as desired)
	Creme Fraiche (to garnish-optional)**

1. Have all ingredients ready before starting.
2. Melt butter in heavy soup pot over high heat.
3. Add squash, onion and shallots and saute until slightly soft, about 7 minutes.
4. Stir in spices and cook for 2 more minutes.
5. Add pumpkin and stock. Cook until squash and onions are thoroughly cooked (about 15 minutes. Season with salt.
6. Remove from heat and puree in blender or processor.

- continued -

94

7. In separate pan, saute carrot, leek, celery and corn, in butter. Add soup puree.
8. Add cream. Serve soup with a dollop of Creme Fraiche on top (optional).

Serves: 6-8
Preparation: 45 minutes

*Julienne is to cut into very thin 1" strips
**A simple Creme Fraiche recipe: mix 1/2 cup cream and 1/2 cup sour cream. Leave out overnight, then refrigerate.

A deliciously hearty soup, perfect for a cold winter's day from Seattle's celebrity chef, Kathy Casey.

HALIBUT WITH GINGER LIME BUTTER

A LA - Fullers

1-1/2	**lbs. fresh halibut** (boned and skinned and cut into four pieces)
	salt and pepper (to taste)
	Ginger-Lime Butter (recipe on next page)
	pickled red ginger (garnish optional)
4	**orange slices**
4	**sprigs cilantro for garnish** (Chinese parsley)
1	**green onion** (green part cut thinly at a slant cut)

1. Cook halibut anyway you prefer; broiled, baked, poached etc.
2. To serve, coat four dinner plates with some of the Ginger-Lime Butter Sauce and place a piece of cooked halibut in center of each one. Top halibut with rest of sauce.
3. Cut red ginger into the shape of 4 small flowers.
4. Garnish each halibut with orange slices, topped with ginger roses and a cilantro sprig.
5. Sprinkle green onion curls around the fish and serve.

Serves: 4
Preparation: 10 minutes

**A simple and *lovely* way to serve halibut. Very tasty!
From chef Kathy Casey.**

96

GINGER-LIME BUTTER SAUCE

A LA - Fullers

1	**T. pickled red ginger** (chopped)*
1/4	**cup sake****
2	**T. rice wine vinegar** (or wine vinegar)
2	**T. orange juice**
1	**T. lime juice**
1	**T. shallot onions** (finely minced)
1	**t. garlic** (finely minced)
1/8	**t. fresh cilantro** (Chinese parsley) (minced)
3/4	**lb. cold unsalted butter** (cut into small cubes)
	salt and pepper (to taste)

1. Combine all except the last 2 ingredients in a heavy saucepan and simmer until liquid is reduced to one to two tablespoons.
2. Turn heat to low and gradually whisk in butter, a few pieces at a time. Keep whisking until all the butter is incorporated into the sauce which will have the consistency of light cream.
3. Strain and season to taste with salt and pepper.
4. Pour over your favorite fish (see recipe previous page).

Yield: enough sauce for 4 fillets
Preparation: 10 minutes

*You'll find pickled red ginger in your bakery section of grocery store.
**If you don't have sake - substitute white wine.

A light "just right" sauce over halibut previous page.

The Georgian

THE GEORGIAN

It's fair to say that The Georgian Room at the Four Seasons Olympic Hotel is one of the most elegant dining rooms in Seattle, with food and service to match.

The Italian Renaissance styled architecture exudes opulence at every turn, from the crystal chandeliers and beautifully paneled walls to the imposing antiques, all against a soft pastel backdrop.

It's not uncommon to see a college class of interior designers peek though the large double doors to view this part of the 1982, $60 million renovation. As you sink into down-filled, silk covered love seats, you'll savor the food which challenges all palatable dreams of lovely ambrosia, exquisitely presented.

We're pleased to share the following recipes from The Georgian, which you'll be proud to serve your guests. Shine your silver and enjoy your finest china and crystal; these recipes are worthy of the best.

The Georgian is located in the Four Seasons Olympic Hotel, 411 University Street, Seattle. Call 621-1700 for reservations.

LAMB CHOPS MARINATED WITH LEMON, GARLIC & ROSEMARY
(Start day ahead - must marinate overnight)

A LA - The Georgian

12	**lamb chops**
1	**T. garlic** (finely chopped)
1	**T. fresh rosemary** (or 1 t. dry)
	salt and pepper (to taste)
4	**T. olive oil** (divided)
3	**whole large lemons** (juiced)

1. Trim lamb chops.
2. Put chops in flat ceramic or glass dish.
3. Sprinkle garlic, rosemary, salt and pepper, and half the olive oil (2 T.) over chops.
4. Add juice from lemons.
5. Make sure all chops have some of all ingredients on them.
6. Cover dish with plastic wrap and refrigerate overnight.
7. Heat heavy pan over high heat. Add remaining olive oil.
8. When oil is hot place chops in pan and cook until both sides are brown, approximately 30-45 <u>seconds</u> per side. Serve immediately.

Serves: 4
Preparation: 7 minutes

This is a wonderfully seasoned medium rare chop. Delicious!

100

ROSEMARY

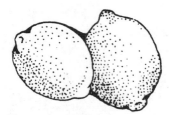

GARLIC

PRAWNS IN BASIL AND GRAIN MUSTARD SAUCE

A LA - The Georgian Room

20	**large prawns** (cleaned and deveined)
	salt and pepper (to taste)
1/2	**cup olive oil** (divided)
1	**T. butter**
1	**T. shallots** (chopped)
1	**cup white wine**
1	**T. grain mustard**
1	**cup whipping cream**
1	**T. fresh basil** (chopped)
4	**fresh basil leaves** (optional)

1. Season prawns with salt and pepper and toss with quarter cup olive oil.
2. Add remaining oil to skillet and cook prawns over medium high heat for one minute.
3. Remove prawns; keep warm.
4. Add butter to skillet; saute shallots until golden brown.
5. Add wine and cook until sauce is reduced to one-third.
6. Add mustard, cream and chopped basil. Bring to a boil. Remove from heat.
7. Combine sauce and prawns.
8. Serve garnished with fresh basil leaf.

Serves: 4
Preparation: 10 minutes

Delicious dish for shrimp or prawns.

Gerard's
Relais de Lyon

Long the vanguard of fine dining in the Seattle area, Gerard's Relais de Lyon in Bothell is an experience not to be missed.

Situated in an elegant country home, exquisitely decorated and set back from the highway, Gerard's makes you feel like you are entering an intimate inn far away from the world's cares. On nice summer evenings you can even have an aperitif or your dinner outside in a lovely courtyard.

Chef owner, Gerard Parrat, is classically trained and served his apprenticeship under the renowned chef, Paul Bocuse, in France. He presents classic French cuisine prepared with skill and imagination and uses Northwest ingredients to make dishes long to be remembered.

Gerard has chosen to share some of his personal favorites with us so that you can create a fine French meal right at home. He is also glad to receive your comments. You may write at his box address below.

Gerard's Relais de Lyon is located at 17121 Bothell Way N.E., Bothell; P.O. Box 733, Bothell 98041. Call 485-7600

103

SEA BASS A LA MARSEILLAISE

A LA - Gerard's Relais de Lyon

2	**lbs. fresh sea bass** or Alaskan jumbo cod (cut into 8 pieces)
2	**T. oil**
1	**cube butter**
1	**T. garlic** (chopped)
2	**T. shallots** (chopped)
1/2	**cup white wine**
1	**cup fish stock** (or clam juice or chicken boullion)
1/2	**cup whipping cream**
2	**T. roux** (1 T. butter blended with 1 T. flour)
	salt and pepper (to taste)

1. Preheat oven to 350º.
2. Over medium-high heat, saute sea bass in oil and half the butter.
3. Season to taste with salt and pepper and finish cooking in 350º oven for 10 minutes
4. In another pan, saute garlic and shallots for about 3 minutes in 1 tablespoon butter.
5. Add wine and stock and reduce by two-thirds, cooking over medium-high heat.
6. Add cream and reduce by half. Add the roux and stir. Boil for 5 minutes.
7. Strain and add remaining butter. Season to taste with salt and pepper. Pour over sea bass and serve immediately.

Serves: 4
Preparation: 35 minutes

Scrumptious!

SALMON WITH BASIL SAUCE

A LA - Gerard's Relais de Lyon

1/4	**cup shallot onions** (minced)
1	**T. butter**
1/4	**cup fresh basil** (chopped)
6	**oz. dry white wine**
1.	**cup fish stock** (or canned clam juice*)
1	**cup heavy cream**
2	**oz. Pernod liqueur**
2	**T. beurre manie** (equal parts flour and butter creamed together)
	salt and pepper (to taste)
4	**salmon fillets**

1. Preheat oven to 325 degrees.
2. In pan over med-high heat, saute shallots in butter until they soften.
3. Add basil and white wine and reduce in half by cooking. Add fish stock and reduce by half again.
4. Add cream and Pernod and reduce again by one third of the volume.
5. Add beurre manie and allow to thicken briefly over lowered heat.
6. Salt and pepper to taste. Set sauce aside and keep warm.
7. Place fillets in oven and bake for 10-13 minutes until meat flakes easily with a fork.
8. Pour sauce over baked salmon and serve.

Serves: 4
Preparation: 15 minutes
Baking: 10-13 minutes

*Clam juice is available in your local grocery.

A delicious way to serve salmon.

106

MINIATURE SCALLOPS IN FENNEL SAUCE

A LA - Gerard's Relais de Lyon

20	**miniature scallops** (rinsed)
4	**shallots** (chopped)
2	**cups dry white wine**
2	**cups fish stock** or clam juice*
4	**T. fresh fennel** (chopped)
1	**cup whipping cream**
	salt and pepper (to taste)
2	**T. Pernod liquour**
2	**tomatoes** (diced)
12	**green onion stems**
8	**miniature carrots** (steamed)

1. Place scallops in a wire steamer.
2. In large kettle combine shallots, wine, fish stock and fennel and bring to a boil.
3. Steam scallops over this stock until done, 2-3 minutes. Remove.
4. Reduce stock mixture to one third by cooking over medium high.
5. Add cream and cook and reduce until mixture coats back of wooden spoon.
6. Season with salt and pepper. Add Pernod.
7. On each serving dish spread sauce. In middle, place 5 scallops.
8. Surround scallops with diced tomatoes.
9. Place green onions in stem shape and use carrots for leaves, so that you have a "flower" on each plate.

Serves: 4 as salad or 1st course
Preparation: 25 minutes

*Clam juice is found in the canned food section of your local grocery.

A showy, delicious beginning to a fancy meal that is easy to fix.

POACHED APPLE IN PASTRY

A LA - Gerard's Relais de Lyon

4	**Criterion apples** (a very sweet green apple)
	Washington State Reisling wine (or other white fruity wine to cover apples)
4	**T. Hazelnut paste***
10	**oz. puff pastry** (ask your bakery or see frozen food section for Fillo dough leaves)
1/2	**cup heavy cream**
8	**mint leaves**

1. Preheat oven to 350 degrees.
2. Peel and core apples.
3. Poach for 10 minutes in simmering wine. Let cool.
4. Fill each apple with 1 tablespoon of Hazelnut paste.
5. Roll puff pastry very thin. (Fillo pastry leaves are ready to use as is). Cut into circles and cover apples top to bottom with pastry.
6. Pierce pastry at top of each apple.
7. Bake in 350º degree oven until golden brown (about 20 minutes).
8. While apples are baking, cook wine over medium heat until it is reduced to a caramel consistency and color.
9. Remove from heat and slowly add the cream, stirring gently. Strain.
10. Cover bottom of warm serving dish with sauce. Place apples in center.
11. Decorate each apple with 2 mint leaves and serve warm.

Serves: 4
Preparation: 30 minutes

*You'll find these pastes in your local grocery store usually in the baking section. Test kitchen also tried Chestnut paste which was very good. Try your favorite.

So delicious, so easy and so lovely!

Gretchen's of Course

206 623-8194

Gretchen's Of Course has long been a name in the forefront of off premise catering in Seattle. Her list of pleased clientele is long and impressive.

When Gretchen Mathers decided to begin offering Seattle office workers the same opportunity to sample high quality food made with care and imagination, she elevated lunch time from the routine to the exciting.

Gretchen's Of Course has two Seattle restaurants open for breakfast and lunch, geared to business and professional people who enjoy exciting food, served casually. The restaurants are famous for their great salad assortment, prepared daily from fresh seasonal ingredients and for fresh baked pastries and desserts. Meals can be eaten inside, outdoors on nice days, or ordered to go.

Gretchen's philosophy has been "to utilize the freshest and finest food stuffs available and to draw from the cuisines of all nations." Her recipes included here reflect that philosophy.

Gretchen's Of Course is located at 1333 Fifth Avenue, Seattle; 623-8194 and 1111 Third Avenue.

109

ZITI SALAD WITH SAUSAGE

A LA - Gretchen's Of Course

12	oz. **Ziti macaroni** or other small pasta
4-6	**quarts boiling salted water**
2	**lbs. smoked farmers sausage** (cooked, thinly sliced)
1	**lb. zucchini** (thinly sliced)
4	**tomatoes** (cut in wedges)
1	**green pepper** (seeded and chopped)
1	**cup parsley** (chopped)
1	**(4 oz.) can chopped pimento**

Ziti Dressing

1-1/3	**cups olive oil**
1/3	**cup red wine vinegar**
1/4	**t. rosemary**
1/4	**t. oregano**
1/4	**t. basil**
1/2	**t. salt**
1/4	**t. pepper**
1/4	**cup grated parmesan**
	lettuce (garnish)

1. Cook macaroni in boiling salted water for 7 minutes or until tender.
2. Drain and rinse with cold water until cool.
3. Combine macaroni, sausage, zucchini, tomatoes, green pepper, parsley and pimento in bowl.

Ziti Dressing

4. Combine olive oil, vinegar, rosemary, oregano, basil, salt, pepper and parmesan. Whisk to blend.
5. Pour over macaroni mixture and gently toss.
6. Serve on lettuce-lined plates.

Serves: 8-10
Preparation: 15 minutes

Test kitchen favorite. Sausage is nice addition. Dressing is light.

110

MANDARIN NOODLE SALAD

A LA - Gretchen's Of Course

1	**lb. wonton mein** (whole egg noodles)
3	**carrots** (julienne cut)*
1	**bunch green onions** (diagonally cut)
1	**cup peanut granules** or 1/2 cup toasted, chopped peanuts (garnish)
	sesame seeds (garnish)

Mandarin Dressing

1/2	**oup dark scsame oil**
1/2	**cup rice vinegar** (in Oriental section of most supermarkets)
1/4	**cup sherry**
1/4	**cup soy sauce**
1	**T. sugar**
1	**T. ginger** (minced)
1	**t. powdered garlic** or 2 cloves (blanched and finely chopped)

1. Cook, rinse and cool noodles. Combine with carrots and onions.

Mandarin Dressing

2. Combine all dressing ingredients and whip with whisk until blended-or put through blender or processor.

3. Pour dressing over noodles, carrots and green onion mix.

4. Add peanut granules and sesame seeds just before serving.

Serves: 4-6
Preparation: 15 minutes

*See *julienne* in Glossary.

A refreshing salad. Perfect for hot summer evenings. Flavors are subtle.

111

MARINATED VEGETABLES

A LA - Gretchen's Of Course

2	**heads cauliflower cut in 1" flowerettes** (blanched* and cooled)
1-1/2	**lbs. broccoli cut in flowerettes** (blanched* and cooled)
1	**lb. carrots cut in 2" sticks** (blanched* and cooled)
1	**lb. zucchini cut in slices** (blanched* and cooled)
1	**lb. brussell sprouts** (blanched* and cooled)
1	**lb. green beans** (blanched* and cooled)
1	**lb. pea pods** (blanched* and cooled)
1	**small red onion** (thinly sliced)
	a lite dressing (use *Zit i Dressing*-recipe next page)

1. Blanch all vegetables except red onion by immersing in salted, boiling water for 1-3 minutes. While still crisp, immerse in cold ice water to stop the cooking. Drain well.
2. Combine all vegetables and red onion with *Ziti Dressing*. Toss and season with salt to taste, if necessary.

Serves: 4-6
Preparation: 5 minutes

*To blanch, immerse vegetables in boiling water for 2 minutes. Then immerse in ice water bath and drain.

Go to the Public Market and purchase your choice of vegetables. This is just a guide.

A great salad!

PASTA PRIMA VERTE

A LA - Gretchen's Of Course

1	lb. fresh linguine pasta
4-6	quarts boiling salted water
10	oz. package frozen peas (rinsed and thawed)
1	lb. broccoli (blanched* and cooled)
1	(4 oz.) can chopped pimento
1/2	cup parsley (chopped)
1-1/2	cups grated parmesan (or more if necessary)
1-1/2	cups half and half (or more if necessary)
1-1/2	t. salt (to taste)
1/2	t. white pepper (to taste)

1. Cut linguine in 6" lengths. Cook in water for 2 minutes**. Do not overcook.
2. Drain and rinse under cold water until cool.
3. Combine linguine, peas, broccoli, pimento, parsley and parmesan.
4. Toss with half and half, seasoned with salt and pepper and serve immediately or chill until ready to serve.

Serves: 4-6 as entree
Preparation: 10 minutes

*To blanch, immerse broccoli in boiling water for 2 minutes. Then immerse in ice water bath and drain.
**If using dry, packaged linguine, cook according to package directions as it will take longer to cook.

A light spring salad, Equally good next day.

113

PARMESAN CHICKEN

A LA - Gretchen's Of Course

1   cup dijon mustard
1/3-1/2 cup white wine
2   cups fresh bread crumbs
2   cups grated parmesan
1   3 lb. fryer (cut up) or 6 chicken breasts

1.   Preheat oven to 375º.
2.   Thin mustard with wine until dipping consistency is
      reached.
3.   Combine bread crumbs and parmesan cheese.
4.   Dip chicken pieces in mustard mix then roll in bread
      crumb mixture.
5.   Place on greased baking sheet.
6.   Bake for 45 minutes or until done.
7.   Serve warm or room temperature.

Serves: 4
Preparation: 10 minutes
Baking: 45 minutes

**A favorite of Gretchen's. Easy to do and great for picnics
or lazy summer days!**

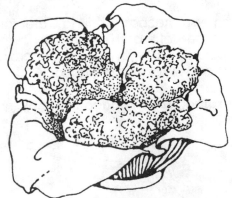

BISCOTTI

A LA - Gretchen's Of Course

1/2	cup butter
1/2	cup sugar
1/2	cup brown sugar
2	large eggs
1	t. vanilla
1/8	cup brandy
1/2	lemon (juice and zest) (see Glossary for *Zest*)
1/8	cup anise seed
4	cups flour
1/2	t. salt
1/2	t. soda
2	t. baking powder
1/2	cup walnuts (chopped)

1. Preheat oven to 350º.
2. Cream butter and sugars until fluffy.
3. Gradually add eggs; then vanilla, brandy, lemon juice and zest and anise. Mix well.
4. Combine flour, salt, soda, baking powder; mix in separate bowl.
5. Add to creamed mixture and blend well.
6. Stir in walnuts.
7. Form dough into two loaves, four inches wide and one inch high.
8. Bake for 25-30 minutes until light brown and springy to touch.
9. Cool slightly. Slice into pieces on slight diagonal and store in airtight container.

Yield: 2 loaves
Preparation: 10 minutes
Baking 30 minutes

A light cookie with slight anise flavor. Perfect with a good cup of coffee anytime or as light dessert with accompaning fruit. Let sit for a couple of days for more anise flavor.

115

DEVONSHIRE CREAM FOR BERRIES

A LA - Gretchen's Of Course

1/2	**lb. cream cheese** (softened)
1/4	**cup confectioners sugar**
1	**t. vanilla**
1	**t. triple sec** (liquor)
1/3	**cup whipping cream**

1. Whip cream cheese and sugar until thoroughly blended.
2. Add vanilla, triple sec and cream.
3. Whip until fluffy.

Yield: 1-1/2 cups
Preparation: 7 minutes

Delicious on fresh local strawberries or blueberries.

Henry's off Broadway

Known as much for its *Travel-Holiday* Magazine award winning cuisine as for its splendid decor, Henry's Off Broadway will delight you at every turn. As soon as the valet parks your car, your cares take leave with him. On a lovely summer day or evening an outdoor terrace beckons as does the sophisticated piano lounge and oyster bar. The versatile entertainment there is among the best in the city. A dining room opulant in crystal, silver, mirrors, green velour, and huge vases of fresh lavender mums sets the stage for excellent continental American cuisine.

Specialties such as Rack of Lamb and Breast of Chicken Calvados dot the menu along with a superb wine selection and luscious desserts.

It is no wonder that Henry's is the choice for those special occasions; you can count on the service and food being extraordinary.

For a rare evening of dining elegance, make reservations and enjoy. The Crystal Room provides privacy and beauty (for groups of up to 24) in a room graced by a hand painted mural by Leo Adams.

Henry's off Broadway is located at 1705 E. Olive Way, Seattle. Call 329-8063 for reservations.

CHICKEN SESAME SALAD

A LA - Henry's Off Broadway

2	**heads romaine lettuce** (cleaned, washed, cores removed and torn in bite-sized pieces)
1-1/2	**cups chicken breast meat** (cooked and sliced julienne* style)
2	**wonton wrappers**** (fried in oil until crisp and crumbled)
1/4	**cup celery** (diced)
1/4	**cup toasted slivered almonds**
1	**T. toasted sesame seeds**
1	**cup *Sweet & Sour Dressing*** (recipe next page)
1	**T. toasted sesame seeds**
1	**large tomato** (cut in wedges)
1	**lemon** (cut in wedges)

1. In large mixing bowl, combine torn lettuce, chicken, wonton wrappers, celery, almonds and 1 tablespoon sesame seeds.
2. Add dressing and toss well.
3. Divide salad onto plates, top with remaining sesame seeds.
4. Garnish with tomatoes and lemons.

Serves: 2 as main course or 4 as 1st course
Preparation: 10 minutes

*See Glossary for *julienne*.
**You'll find wonton wrappers in your local grocery store. Just ask for them.

Wonderful flavor combination. A must try.

118

SWEET AND SOUR DRESSING

A LA - Henry's Off Broadway

2	cups sugar
4	t. Colman's Dry Mustard
1-1/2	cups rice-wine vinegar
2	T. soy sauce
2	t. fresh ginger (peeled & grated)
1	clove garlic (minced)
2	T. Sesame oil
4	T. vegetable oil
1	T. lemon juice
1-1/2	t. salt
2	t. cracked black pepper

1. Combine sugar and mustard.
2. Slowly add vinegar, stirring until mixture has a smooth consistency.
3. Place mixture in top of double boiler. Cook and stir until sugar dissolves.
4. Stir in soy sauce, ginger and garlic. Blend well.
5. Add both oils, lemon juice, salt and pepper.
6. Remove from stove; cool and refrigerate at least 4 hours so flavors blend.
7. Stir well before using.

Yield: 3 cups
Preparation: 10 minutes

Serve with *Chicken Sesame Salad* or any hearty combination of greens and meat. Delicious!

119

THYME

BASIL

GARLIC

BLACK TIE TOMATO SOUP

A LA - Henry's Off Broadway

8-10	**tomatoes** (peeled and seeded)
1/2	**t. sugar**
1/2	**t. salt**
1/2	**t. black pepper**
1	**large clove garlic** (peeled and minced)
3	**T. butter**
1	**cup fresh mushrooms** (finely sliced)
1	**pinch whole thyme** (chopped)
2	**pinches whole basil** (chopped)
3	**strips cooked bacon** (crisp and crumbled)
1	**T. gin**
1/2	**cup** (or more) **whipping cream**
	whipping cream and green onions (optional garnish)

1. Puree tomatoes in blender or food processor.
2. Add sugar, salt, pepper and *one half* of the the garlic to tomatoes and blend well.
3. Melt butter in fry pan over medium-high heat, and add mushrooms,remaining garlic, thyme and basil. Cook until mushrooms are just done and add bacon.
4. Add gin to mushrooms and ignite.* Reduce to low heat ; add tomato mixture and blend well.
5. Pour in cream and simmer 20 minutes (add more cream if soup is too thick).
6. Garnish each bowl if you like with unsweetened whipped cream and thinly sliced green onions.

Serves: 4 as appetizer
Preparation: 30 minutes
Cooking: 20 minutes to simmer

*See *flamber* in Glossary

One of the most delicious soups we've tasted. A sure hit!

BREAST OF CHICKEN CALVADOS

A LA - Henry's Off Broadway

4	**medium boned chicken breasts**
	flour (seasoned with salt and pepper)
2	**oz. butter** (or more to saute)
16	**thin apple slices**
1/2	**cup apple juice**
1-1/2	**cups chicken stock** (bouillion)
1/2	**cup cream**
3	**T. Calvados brandy** (or other brand)

1. Dust chicken breasts in light coating of seasoned flour. Saute in butter until brown on both sides.
2. Add sliced apples, apple juice, chicken stock and cream.
3. Cook over medium heat until sauce is reduced in half (about 15 minutes-sauce will turn a caramel color).
4. Stir in brandy and serve.

Serves: 4
Preparation: 35 minutes

So easy and delicious. Test kitchen recommends serving with broccoli and pouring sauce over all.

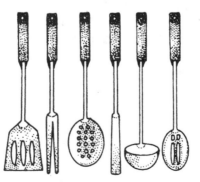

Hiram's
At·The·Locks

Boating is one of Seattle's favorite activities, whether you are participating or just watching. Hiram's at the Locks is the perfect place to enjoy the excitement of this sport, which takes place year 'round at the Hiram Chittenden Locks.

Hiram's is a 175 seat restaurant located just above the Locks and is a favorite spot for Sunday brunch, a drink on the patio on a summer afternoon or dinner when the locks are lighted. Boats and water offer a perfect back drop for delicious Northwest cuisine.

Hiram's features fresh seasonal seafood specialties, mesquite broiled steaks and veal dishes all carefully prepared. Some test kitchen favorites included in this book, are: Halibut Brie with Toasted Pecans, Veal Grand Marnier and Strawberries Amaretto. Try these recipes at home and capture the feeling of a leisurely meal in front of one of Seattle's favorite scenes.

Hiram's is located at 5300 34th N.W. in Seattle. Call 784-1733 for reservations.

123

OYSTERS CHITTENDEN

A LA - Hiram's at the Locks

12	**Quilcene oysters** (shucked-save all the half shells)
1/4	**cup olive oil**
1/4	**cup onion** (diced)
1/4	**cup green pepper** (diced)
1/4	**cup mushrooms** (sliced)
2	**cloves garlic** (minced)
1/2	**cup tomato sauce**
1	**t. tabasco sauce**
1	**t. fresh basil (**chopped)
	salt (to taste)
1/4	**cup Asiago cheese** (grated)*

1. Place oysters on half-shell. Set aside.
2. In heavy pan, heat oil. Add onions, green peppers mushrooms & garlic.
3. Saute until green peppers become soft.
4. Add tomato sauce, tabasco & basil; bring to boil.
5. Salt to taste.
6. Fill each oyster with sauce and cover with cheese.
7. Place oysters on broiler pan and bake at 400º for 6-8 minutes.

Serves: 2
Preparation: 20 minutes

*Available at Safeway Supermarkets or substitute Romano Cheese.

Wonderful flavor combination. A must for oyster lovers!

PRAWNS VICTORIA

A LA - Hiram's at the Locks

1/8	**cup clarified butter**
1/2	**cup flour**
14	**medium prawns** (peeled and deveined)
2	**cloves shallots** (minced)
1	**clove garlic** (minced)
1/2	**cup red onion** (thinly sliced)
1	**cup small button mushrooms**
1/2	**cup sour cream**
1	**cup whipping cream**
1/2	**cup champagne**
	salt (to taste)

1. Heat butter in heavy saute pan over medium high.
2. Dust prawns in flour.
3. Cook prawns, shallots, garlic, onion and mush-rooms until prawns turn pink.
4. Add sour cream and whipping cream.
5. Bring to a boil and reduce liquid by one third by cooking.
6. Add champagne and salt and serve immediately.

Serves: 2
Preparation: 10 minutes

A wonderful rich meal!

125

PROVIMI VEAL GRAND MARNIER

A LA - Hiram's at the Locks

1/4	**cup clarified butter***
12	**oz. veal** **(trimmed and pounded)
1/4	**cup flour**
4	**large prawns** (peeled and deveined)
1	**shallot onion** (minced)
1/4	**large lemon**
1/4	**large orange**
1/4	**cup Grand Marnier liqueur**

1. Heat butter in heavy saute or frying pan.
2. Cut veal in 4 equal portions; dust in flour, shaking off excess.
3. Saute veal over high heat for 1 minute, browning on both sides.
4. Remove from pan and keep warm.
5. Add prawns; shallots; juices from lemon and orange; and Grand Marnier.
6. Cook until sauce thickens slightly.
7. Pour sauce over veal. Serve immediately.

Serves: 2
Preparation: 5 minutes

*See Glossary for *clarified* butter.
**Hirams uses Provimi veal from Provimi, Wisconson, a top-of-the-line milk fed veal.

A delicious combination! Shows off veal well!

HALIBUT BRIE
WITH TOASTED PECANS

A LA - Hirams at the Locks

1	lb. fresh halibut fillets or chunks
1/2	cup flour
1	T. clarified butter*
3/4	cup whipping cream
1/4	lb. Brie (cut into pieces)
1/8	cup white wine
1/4	cup toasted pecans

1. Dust halibut in flour. Shake off excess.
2. Heat butter in saute pan.
3. Add halibut and saute until golden brown on both sides.
4. Add whipping cream and brie pieces.
5. Bring to boil and reduce by one third by cooking until sauce thickens, approximately 2-3 minutes.
6. Add wine and serve topped with pecans.

Serves: 2 generously
Preparation: 10 minutes

*See Glossary for *clarified*.

**A wonderful way to serve fresh halibut.
A favorite of the test kitchen.**

STRAWBERRIES AMARETTO

A LA - Hirams at the Locks

1	pint fresh strawberries
1	cup whipping cream
3	oz. amaretto
2	T. toasted almonds

1. Rinse strawberries; drain until dry.
2. Cut off stems and slice in half.
3. Place in two serving bowls.
4. Whip cream until firm peaks form.
5. Carefully fold in amaretto and pour over berries.
6. Top with almonds and serve.

Serves: 2
Preparation: 10 minutes

**A must for fresh Northwest berries in June!
Yummy!**

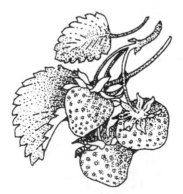

Hogan's BAY CO.

In 1984, Walter "Mickey" Hogan purchased what is now Hogan's Bay Co., formerly known as Clinkerdaggers's.

This olde English inn type of place is an inviting retreat, sitting atop rugged pilings on Puget Sound. It's complete with gridded windows, hanging potted flowers and a sheltered walk.

A marvelously comfortable interior greets you with its glowing fire, a welcomed warmth on cold, damp nights. In this cozy eating establishment, you'll sink into high backed chairs, flame stitched in blue and cream on a blue and rose carpet, flanked by eggnog colored walls.

Enjoy great food for lunch, dinner and Sunday Brunch. Topping the menu list in popularity are the Prime Rib, Halibut Rainier and Seafood Fettuccine. The all time favorite dessert and by far the best in the "kingdom" is their Burnt Cream, which recipe we're proud to include in this book.

The Bay Co. is located at 3327 Ruston Way, Tacoma. Call 752-6661 for reservations.

BURNT CREAM

A LA - Hogan's Bay Co.

1	pint whipping cream
4	egg yolks
1/2	cup granulated sugar
1	T. vanilla
4	T. sugar
1	t. brown sugar

1. Preheat oven to 350º. Heat cream over low heat until bubbles form around edge of pan.
2. Beat egg yolks and sugar together until thick, about 3 minutes.
3. Gradually beat cream into egg yolk mixture.
4. Stir in vanilla.
5. Pour custard into six (6 oz.) custard cups.
6. Place cups in shallow baking pan.
7. Pour 1/2 inch water in bottom.
8. Bake until set; approximately 25 minutes.
9. Remove cups and refrigerate until chilled.
10. Combine white and brown sugars. Sprinkle 2 teaspoons over each custard.
11. Place on top rack of broiler. Broil until topping is medium brown.
12. Chill before serving.

Serves: 6
Preparation: 45 minutes
Refrigeration: 2 hours

A rich dessert and long time favorite at Hogan's Bay Company. Very easy!

131

HALIBUT RAINIER

A LA - Hogan's Bay Co.

4	**(6 oz.) halibut steaks** or filets
1/2	**cup butter** (melted)
1/2	**cup lemon juice**
1/2	**cup sour cream**
1/2	**cup cheddar cheese**
1/2	**cup bay shrimp** or shrimp meat

1. Preheat oven 350º. Place halibut in shallow baking dish.
2. Combine melted butter and lemon juice and pour over fish.
3. Bake for 10-15 minutes or until fish is cooked and flakes easily. Do not over-cook or it will be dry.
4. Remove from oven.
5. Top each steak with sour cream, cheddar cheese and shrimp.
6. Broil just until cheese melts.

Serves: 4
Preparation: 20 minutes

A moist dish with great flavor. Try topping on other white fish.

Hunt Club Room

Escape from the ordinary; come to the Hunt Club Room at the Sorrento Hotel. Enjoy fresh continental fare, featuring regional specialties with a touch of nouvelle cuisine. Owing to creative chefs, you'll sample Spring Soup with Snap Peas and Dungeness Crab, Roast Oregon Quail with Rhubarb Chutney and such rarities as Oriental Steamed Lamb Dumplings with Mustard Greens and Cilantro. Add to this a spectacular Squid Salad, a sizeable wine list and fresh homemade pastries, and you'll find an exceptional restaurant.

Built in 1908 in Renaissance style after a castle in Sorrento, the hotel's tasteful elegance will remind you of a time and place where tradition and beauty abounded. The Hunt Club's dark Honduras mahogany paneled room is divided into intimately quiet sections that invite conversation. Service is attentive and knowledgable. In an atmosphere of discreet luxury you'll savor the coziness and English flavor of the Hunt Club or relax in the Fireside Lobby with a piano and a Rookwood fireplace. For true romantics there is a tile paved courtyard complete with Italian fountain and open air seating for the summer months. Guests have been known to hail requests to the piano player below from their courtyard windows on a warm summer's eve.

The trappings of modern living take leave as soon as the valet parks your car and you escape to extraordinary dining.

Located at 900 Madison Ave., Seattle.   Call 622-6400 for reservations.

133

SPRING SOUP WITH SUGARSNAP PEAS & CRAB

A LA - Hunt Club Room

1	**medium onion** (chopped)
1	**stalk celery** (chopped)
2	**carrots** (chopped)
4	**shallots** (chopped)
1	**leek** (chopped)
1	**cup mushrooms** (chopped)
2	**sprigs thyme** (or 1/2 t. dry)
2	**sprigs tarragon** (or 1/2 t. dry)
4	**cloves garlic** (chopped)
2	**qts. chicken stock or broth**
1	**lb. sugar snap peas** (blanched, coarsly chopped)
	salt and pepper (to taste)

Garnish
1	**carrot** (fine julienne cut*)
1	**leek** (fine julienne cut*)
1	**stalk celery** (fine julienne cut*)
1	**medium zucchini** (remove core & fine julienne*)
1	**medium yellow squash**
12	**pieces crabmeat** (cooked)
6	**snap peas** (blanched)
6	**squash blossoms** (optional)
	lemon juice (to taste)

1. Combine onions, celery, carrots, shallots, leek and mushrooms in large heavy sauce pan.
2. Stir over low heat without browning.
3. Add thyme, tarragon, garlic. Cook until transparent.
4. Pour in chicken stock. Bring to a boil over high heat.
5. Reduce heat to simmer and cook until liquid is reduced by half.
6. Strain broth through fine sieve. Press all liquid out of vegetables.

- continued -

7. Puree peas in food processor with 1 cup stock until very smooth.
8. Add puree to stock and heat. Do not boil. Season to taste with salt and pepper.

Garnish
9. Divide julienne vegetables among 6 wide rimmed soup bowls. Add crab meat.
10. Pour hot soup over vegetables. Float 1 blossom and 1 snap pea on top and a dash of lemon juice to your taste and serve.

Serves: 6
Preparation: 45 minutes

*See Glossary for *Julienne* cut.

Tastes like you're eating peas fresh out of the garden! A very colorful way to begin a meal.

TRIPLE CHOCOLATE CAKE

A LA - Hunt Club Room

6	**oz. semi-sweet chocolate*** (chopped into small pieces)
6	**oz. bittersweet chocolate*** (chopped into small pieces)
4	**oz. unsweetened chocolate** (chopped into small pieces)
1	**cup water**
1/2	**cup granulated sugar**
1/2	**cup butter**
8	**eggs** (separated)
1	**cup almonds** (ground to fine dry powder)
1/4	**cup powdered sugar** (garnish)
	shaved chocolate (garnish)

1. Preheat oven to 300º. Butter and flour 10" spring-form pan.
2. Place chocolate in a 3 quart bowl with water and sugar.
3. Microwave for 1-2 minutes until chocolate is melted or place in double boiler over hot, but not boiling water and melt.
4. In medium stainless mixing bowl cream butter until smooth, but not whitened.
5. Slowly add egg yolks, one at a time, beating well after each addition.
6. When eggs are well incorporated, add almonds and mix until combined.
7. Slowly add melted chocolate mixture; mix until well blended.
8. Whip egg whites until barely soft peaks form.
9. Fold one third of whipped whites into chocolate.
10. Fold remaining whites in 3 batches being careful not to over-mix.

- continued -

11. Pour mixture into prepared spring-form pan.
12. Place in a watertight container, pour cold water half-way up side of cake pan.
13. Bake for 2 hours in oven. Remove from oven; allow to cool to room temperature in water bath.
14. When cool, remove from water bath, and cool on wire rack.
15. Refrigerate 6 hours or overnight.
16. Dust with powdered sugar and a sprinkling of chocolate shavings.

Serves: 12
Preparation: 30 minutes
Baking: 2 hours
Refrigerate: 6 hours or overnight

*Peters brand Semi-Sweet Chocolate and Guittard brand Bittersweet Chocolate are recommended.

A sinfully rich, chocolate cake. A must for chocolate lovers!

FETTUCCINE WITH PINK SCALLOPS AND CHANTERELLES

A LA - Hunt Club Room

16	**pink scallops** or other scallop
2	**T. white wine**
2	**cups chanterelles** (sliced) or other fresh mushroom
1	**t. peanut oil**
2	**T. Marsala wine**
2	**tomatoes** (cooked, seeded and chopped)
1	**T. cream**
1/2	**cup butter**
1	**lb. fettuccine** (cooked and warm)
1/4	**cup chives** (minced)

1. If using pink scallops, wash well. Place in skillet with lid; add wine.
2. Steam over medium-high heat until shells open.
3. Remove from pan and keep scallops warm. Reserve any liquid for later use. (If using shelled scallops, cook until done)
4. Saute chanterelles in peanut oil.
5. Add Marsala and deglaze pan by scraping up residue at bottom while cooking.
6. Add reserved scallop liquid and chopped tomatoes.
7. Cook until reduced by half.
8. Add cream and bring to boil
9. Over low heat, whip in butter a little bit at a time until well incorporated.
10. Remove from heat.
11. Toss fettuccine in chanterelle, tomato mixture.
12. Divide between 4 wide-rimmed soup bowls or plates.
13. Add warm scallops to the side and garnish with minced chives.

Serves: 4
Preparation: 15 minutes

A colorful and flavorful pasta dish. Try for raves at your next festive meal.

138

Ask Seattleites why they come to Jake's and many will extol
the virtues of the best prime rib in town; others rave about the
fresh jumbo prawns and live lobster and then there is a very
special group of connoisseurs who come for the spectacular
bar. Yes, there are twelve different varieties of draught beer
from around the world, plus the largest collection of single-
malt Scotches in the world, three dozen cognacs, Guinness
Stout on tap and a singing bartender, Robert Julien.

Add to this a friendly and knowledgeable staff and you've
got a winning restaurant worthy of your patronage. Noted in
the Mobil Travel Guide year after year, Jake's is consistent in
quality, freshness and service, and all this at reasonable
prices.

Come for a hearty portion of the blending of Seattle hospital-
ity and a bit o' Irish cheer.

Jake O'Shaughnessey's is located at 100 Mercer Street,
Seattle. Call 285-1897 for reservations. There is a second
location in Bellevue Square, Bellevue. Call 455-5559 for reservations.

HOUSE WILTED SALAD

A LA - Jake O'Shaughnessey

Dressing
6   strips bacon
2   T. sugar
3   T. red wine vinegar
1   t. Worchestershire Sauce
1/2   t. dry mustard
       salt and pepper (to taste)

Salad
1/2   head romaine lettuce (torn into bite-size pieces)
1   T. black olives (chopped)
2   T. scallions (finely diced)
2   T. hard boiled egg (chopped)
2   T. toasted, slivered almonds (garnish)

Dressing
1   Cook bacon until crisp. Drain on towels and then crumble bacon. Set aside. Discard all but four tablespoons of drippings.
2.   In same pan, stir together sugar, vinegar, Worchestershire Sauce, dry mustard and four tablespoons drippings. Whisk until it's emulsified.
3.   Cook over medium heat and continue to stir until heated throughly. Add salt and pepper to taste. Set aside.

Salad
4.   Place lettuce in salad bowl. Top with olives, scallions and egg. Drizzle warm dressing over salad. Add reserved bacon and toss thoroughly. Top with almonds.

Serves: 4
Preparation: 15 minutes   **Yummy!**

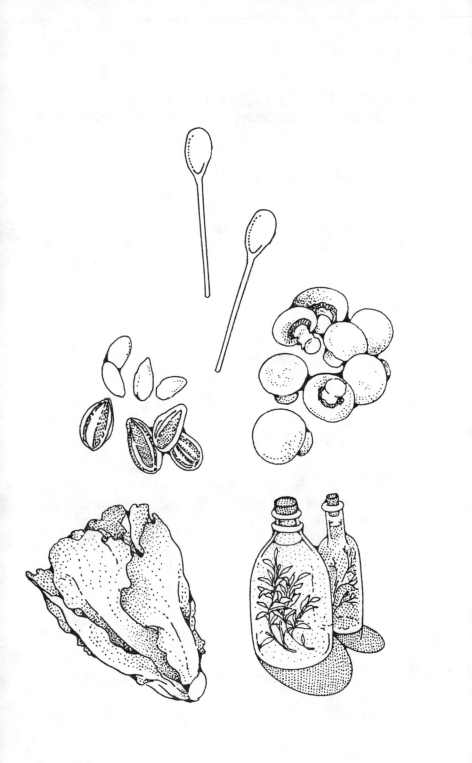

MARINATED GRILLED SHRIMP

A LA - Jake O'Shaughnessey's

Other Ingredients
wooden skewers (8"-10") one for every 4 shrimp
2   **lbs. shrimp in shell** (16-20 count per pound)
       citrus fruit (lemons, limes and oranges) (cut into 1/2"
       thick wedges; three wedges per every four shrimp)

Marinade
1   **cup salad oil**
1   **cup lemon juice**
1/4   **cup soy sauce**
2   **T. fresh parsley** (minced)
4   **t. tarragon leaves**
1/2   **t. chervil** (minced)
1/4   **t. basil** (minced)
2   **garlic cloves** (peeled and minced)
1/2   **t. salt**
4   **peppercorns** (crushed)

1.   Soak the skewers in water for at least one hour before
       assembling. This prevents the wood from catching on
       fire when placed on the grill.
2.   While skewers are soaking, use a pair of small scissors
       or a sharp knife to cut a slit along the back of the
       shrimp, from head to tail. This incision allows you to
       devein the shrimp, and also makes it easier to peel off
       the shell after cooking. It is important to grill the shrimp
       with the shell on so that the juices are sealed in and the
       shrimp is more flavorful.

Marinade
3.   Combine and thoroughly mix the marinade ingredi-
       ents.

- continued -

4. Assemble skewers in this order: shrimp, citrus, shrimp, citrus, shrimp, citrus, shrimp. There are a total of four shrimp and three citrus wedges per skewer. Skewer the shrimp twice, once through the tail, and again through the thick part (head) so that the shrimp is curled around the skewer in a "U".

5. Place assembled skewers in one layer on the bottom of a non-metallic pan. Pour the marinade over the skewers and marinate for 2-3 hours, turning in pan once an hour.

6. Grill skewers for 2-3 minutes each side until the shrimp are pink and opaque. Do not overcook.

7. Serve immediately over a bed of *Lemon Pilaf*. (Recipe next page).

Serves:4-6
Preparation: 25 minutes
Marination: 2-3 hours

Great as appetizer or entree!

LEMON PILAF

A LA - Jake O'Shaughnessey's

1/4	**cup butter**
1	**cup onion** (minced 1/4" pieces)
1	**t. garlic** (finely minced)
2	**cups long grain white rice**
1/2	**cup fresh lemon juice**
1/4	**cup fresh parsley** (minced)
1	**t. thyme**
1/2	**t. basil**
1/2	**t. dill weed**
1/2	**t. salt**
1/4	**t. freshly ground pepper**
1/2	**cup grated parmesan**
2-3/4	**cups Swanson's chicken stock** (heated to boiling)

1. Preheat oven to 350º.
2. Heat butter over medium heat in a large kettle. When melted, add the onion and garlic, taking care not to over-brown, stirring frequently.
3. After 2-3 minutes, add rice to onion mixture, tossing grains well to coat with butter. Saute for 1-2 minutes more.
4. Add lemon juice, parsley, herbs, spices, cheese and boiling chicken broth. (The broth must be hot to produce a fluffy, light pilaf. Cold liquid tends to produce a soggy, heavy final product). Stir well.
5. Cover well with lid, place in 350º oven and bake for 20 minutes. After 20 minutes, rice should be done: no liquid in the bottom of the pan, rice fluffy and tender. If rice is still crunchy, bake for an additional 5 minutes (you may need to add a little more hot broth).

- continued -

6.   Remove from oven. Fluff the rice up with two large forks (preferably) or carefully, two large cook's spoons. Be sure that any herbs that may have floated to the top are gently folded into the body of the rice.
7.   Serve immediately.

Serves: 8
Preparation: 30 minutes

Yummy!

Le Provencal

Le Provençal

In the early 1970's, dining out in Seattle meant deep-fried seafood or steak served in dark restaurants.

When Philippe Gayte opened Le Provencal in 1973, he was going against prevailing trends; he chose to open a casual bistro style restaurant featuring good food and the flavor of Southern France, his birth place. Located in Kirkland, the restaurant exudes a bright, Mediterranean decor. The food is classic French, lightened by the use of fresh Northwest ingredients. It has long been a popular place to go for special events and delicious lunches and dinners.

Now you can savor the sunshine of Southern France anytime by preparing Chicken with Red Pepper Sauce, Rabbit in Cream, or Floating Island, a favorite French way to end a meal.

Le Provencal is located at 212 Central Way, Kirkland. Call 827-3300 for reservations.

147

RABBIT A LA CREME

A LA - Le Provencal

6	**T. butter**
2	**rabbits** (cut up)
1	**cup onion** or 2 shallots (chopped)
1	**pint whipping cream**
	pinch of Bouquet Garni*
	salt and pepper (to taste)
6	**T. fresh parsley** (chopped)

1. Melt butter in saute pan over medium heat. Saute rabbit pieces in butter with onion or shallots for 15 minutes.
2. Turn rabbit pieces so they don't color too much.
3. Add cream and a pinch of Bouquet Garni*,and salt and pepper. Cook slowly for 18-20 minutes.
4. Remove rabbit to serving dish; keep warm.
5. Strain sauce over meat. Sprinkle with parsley.
6. Serve immediately.

Serves: 4
Preparation: 45 minutes

*Bouquet Garni is a mixture of herbs. It's commonly found in your grocery's spice section.

A wonderful way to cook rabbit. This dish is delicious with fresh pasta. During the fall, serve with Chanterelle mushrooms (in season then) sauteed in olive oil, garlic and parsley.

SUPREME OF CHICKEN WITH RED PEPPER SAUCE

A LA - Le Provencal

Red Pepper Sauce

1	**T. butter**
2	**shallots** (chopped)
1/2	**cup dry white wine**
1	**chicken bouillon cube**
1	**cup whipping cream**
1	**small red pepper** (blanched* and cooled)
	salt and pepper (to taste)

1	**T. butter**
4	**boneless, skinless chicken breasts**

Red Pepper Sauce

1. Melt 1 tablespoon butter in small saucepan over low heat. Saute shallots but do not brown.
2. Add wine and chicken cube and reduce by half by cooking.
3. Add cream. Cook, stirring constantly, for 8 minutes.
4. Julienne** red pepper and add to sauce. Taste and add salt and pepper if desired. Cook for additional 4 minutes. Set sauce aside and keep hot.

5. In large saute pan, melt 1 tablespoon butter over low. Heat and saute chicken slowly until lightly browned and done, approximately 10 minutes.
6. Serve immediately topped with Red Pepper Sauce.

Serves: 4
Preparation: 25 minutes

*To blanch, drop in boiling water 1 minute.
**See how to *julienne* in Glossary

A colorful dish with a wonderful taste!

FLOATING ISLAND

A LA - Le Provencal

Meringues
3   **egg whites**
1/4   **cup sugar**
2   **cups milk** (scalded)
Custard
3   **egg yolks**
1/4   **cup sugar**
1/8   **t. salt**
2   **cups milk**
1   **t. vanilla** (can substitute rum, dry sherry or a little grated lemon rind).

Meringues
1.   Whip the egg whites until stiff and gradually beat in sugar.
2.   Scald milk in pan on burner turned to simmer.
3.   Drop the meringue mixture from a tablespoon into the scalded milk and poach them gently at a simmer for about 4 minutes, turning them once.
4.   Take them out carefully with a slotted spoon into a towel.
5.   Save milk to make custard.
      Custard
6.   Beat slightly, 3 egg yolks. Add sugar and salt.
7.   Slowly stir in milk. Cook very slowly to prevent curdling (*Do Not* let it boil)until mixture begins to thicken. Cool.
8.   Add vanilla.
9.   Serve custard in low dish with meringues floating on top or individually in a stemmed glass with meringue on top.

Serves: 4-6 (about 20-25 meringues)
Preparation: 30 minutes
This is a delicate French dessert called Oeufs A 'La Neige or "Eggs In Snow".

150

Le Tastevin in French means "the wine tasting cup." In Seattle it means the melding of fine food and wine in a light relaxing atmosphere with the Space Needle overhead and Puget Sound over your shoulder.

Having opened their restaurant in 1976, Emile Ninaud, Wine Merchant, and Jacques Boiroux, Executive Chef, have given Seattleites a place to enjoy finely prepared Northwest specialties such as Salmon, Crab, Hama Hama Oysters and Penn Cove Mussels along with fine Northwest wines from Columbia Crest, St. Michelle, and Hinzerling. Also included are fine European varietals and Spanish sherries.

Located near the Seattle Center, Le Tastevin enjoys a clientele that frequents the Opera, Seattle Repertory Theater, A.C.T., and the Sonics, as well as the Pacific Science Center, which is the location of meetings of the Seattle Chapter of Les Amis du Vin. It is a consistent award winner in many dining categories.

Jacques Boiroux has chosen to share recipes that reflect his wide range of culinary interest, in addition to making use of the Northwest's finest fresh ingredients and wines. Make your next meal a delight at Le Tastevin.

Le Tastevin is located at 19 W. Harrison, Seattle. Call 283-0991 for reservations.

151

MUSHROOM SALAD WITH VINAIGRETTE DRESSING

(Begin 1 hour ahead)

A LA - Le Tastevin

1/4	**lb. large white mushrooms** (sliced)
1/4	**lb. Shitake mushrooms** (sliced)*
1/4	**lb. Enoki mushrooms***
	juice of 1/2 lemon
1	**T. chives** (chopped)
3	**T. white wine vinegar**
1	**T. Dijon mustard**
1/2	**cup olive oil**
	salt and pepper (to taste)
8	**cherry tomatoes**
8	**calamata olives** or other large black brine-cured olive

1. Combine all mushrooms and toss with lemon juice and chives.
2. In separate bowl, blend vinegar and mustard with whisk or use processer.
3. Gradually add oil in a light stream, beating constantly until dressing thickens.
4. Season to taste with salt and pepper.
5. Add to mushrooms. Toss and chill for 1 hour.
6. Garnish with cherry tomatoes and olives.

Serves: 4 as salad
Preparation: 10 minutes
Refrigeration: 1 hour

*Try it with all white mushrooms if Shitakes and Enokis are not available.

This salad is great as a first course or accompaniment to chicken or fish.

152

HAMMA-HAMMA OYSTERS WITH CAPERS & ENOKI MUSHROOMS

A LA - Le Tastevin

24	**freshly shucked oysters**
1	**cup flour**
3	**eggs** (beaten)
3	**t. corn oil**
1/2	**cup butter**
1/2	**cup capers**
1/4	**lb. Enoki mushrooms**
2	**lemons**
1/2	**bunch cilantro** (Chinese parsley-optional)

1. Dust oysters in flour and dip in egg.
2. Add corn oil to hot skillet.
3. Pan fry oysters until golden brown on both sides. Leave in pan.
4. Drain any excess oil. Add butter to hot pan in small pieces.
5. Put in capers, mushrooms and juice of one lemon. Cook for two minutes.
6. Serve at once on warm plates, garnished with lemon wedges and cilantro sprigs.

Serves: 4
Preparation: 20 minutes

A must for all oyster lovers!

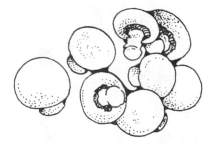

MUSSELS POULETTE

A LA - Le Tastevin

4	**lbs. mussels** (scrubbed)
2	**shallots** (finely chopped)
1	**cup Semillon wine** (or any white wine)
1	**cup whipping cream**
4	**T. butter**
	pepper (to taste)
2	**T. cilantro** (Chinese parsley) chopped

1. In large saucepan, place mussels, shallots and wine.
2. Over high heat bring to boil until mussels open up, approximately five minutes.
3. Remove mussels, and remove top shell, so that you have mussels on half-shell.
4. Put mussels in warm soup bowls and keep warm.
5. Add cream to sauce pan. Over high heat, reduce by half.
6. Slowly add butter, by tablespoons, until all is incorporated.
7. Season to taste with pepper.
8. Pour sauce evenly over mussels. (If sauce is too thin, add a little cornstarch diluted in water).
9. Garnish with cilantro and serve.

Serves: 4 as main course; 6-8 as appetizer
Preparation: 30 minutes

A wonderful treat! Serve with sourdough bread and a crisp green salad.

154

LING COD AU GEWURZTAMINER BEURRE BLANC

A LA - Le Tastevin

2	**cups Gewurztraminer wine** (white wine)
2	**shallots** (chopped)
1/4	**cup whipping cream**
1/2	**lb. of butter** (softened)
	cayenne (to taste)
	juice of 1/2 lemon (or to taste)
6	**(6 oz) fillets of Ling Cod** (or Sea Bass or Red Snapper)
1/2	**cup flour**(seasoned with pinch of paprika, garlic salt and celery salt)
1/4	**cup corn oil**

1. Preheat oven to 350º.
2. In an enamel or stainless saucepan combine wine and shallots over medium high heat. Cook until reduced by half.
3. Add cream; simmer for 5 minutes over low heat.
4. Add butter by teaspoonfuls, whisking constantly until butter is well incorporated.
5. Season to taste with cayenne pepper and lemon juice.
6. Flour fillets; dust off excess.
7. Heat oil over medium high heat and fry fillets until lightly browned.
8. Finish by baking in oven for 5 minutes.
9. Pour one third sauce on bottom of platter. Arrange fillets on top. Drizzle with more sauce and serve. Serve remaining sauce in gravy boat.

Serves: 6
Preparation: 15 minutes

A light entree with great flavor! Try it! At Le Tastevin this dish is garnished with lemon wedges; cilantro sprigs; and Chanterelle mushrooms which have been sauteed in butter, minced garlic and dill.

LAMB FILETS WITH CALAMATA OLIVE SAUCE

A LA - Le Tastevin

2	**T. butter**
2	**T. olive oil**
6	**lamb filets** or 12 thin lamb chops
	salt and pepper
1	**T. butter**
3	**T. shallot onions** (finely chopped)
1	**cup full bodied red wine**
1/2	**cup beef broth**
1	**small bay leaf**
	pinch of thyme
24	**black Calamata olives** or Greek olives (pitted and sliced)
1/8	**cup cognac**

1. Heat butter and olive oil in heavy skillet until foam from butter subsides.
2. Add filets or chops and saute 30 seconds on each side. Transfer to heated platter. Salt and pepper to taste and keep warm.
3. In same skillet, melt one tablespoon of butter; add shallots and cook for 2 minutes over medium heat.
4. Add wine, broth, bay leaf and thyme.
5. Increase heat to medium high and cook, stirring to scrape up pan drippings until liquid is reduced to 3/4 cups, approximately 4-5 minutes.
6. Remove from heat. Stir in olives and cognac.
7. Remove bay leaf; season with salt and pepper to taste.

- continued -

8.   Coat bottom of plates with sauce.
9.   Slice filets into 5 slices and arrange in attractive manner and serve.

Serves; 6
Preparation: 15 minutes

Unusual way to serve lamb. A must for all lamb lovers!

CHOCOLATE SORBET

A LA - Le Tastevin

4	oz. unsweetened chocolate
1	qt. water
1-1/2	cups sugar
	fresh mint for garnish (optional)

1. Chop chocolate into small pieces.
2. Heat water and sugar over medium heat in heavy sauce pan until sugar dissolves.
3. Add chocolate: simmer until mixture is smooth.
4. Turn heat down very low. Simmer mixture for 10 minutes. Do Not Boil.
5. Remove from heat and cool to room temperature.
6. Pour mixture into freezer container and freeze as you would any other ice cream.*
7. Serve garnished with a sprig of fresh mint.

Serves: 4 to 6 people, two scoops each
Preparation: 15 minutes plus freezing time

*Preferably you would do this in an ice-cream maker. There are many inexpensive and easy ones on the market. If you do not have an ice-cream maker, you can freeze ice-cream until ice crystals form (20 minutes). Then stir the ice-cream and freeze again, repeating the freeze, stir, freeze, stir process for several hours.

A delicious chocolate dessert. Try with different types of chocolate for variety.

In a city renowned for its fresh seafood, The Leschi Lakecafe has made a name for itself by serving very fresh seafood complemented with delicious sauces.

A 400 gallon tank displays live seafood such as lobster, crab and bags of oysters, clams and scallops. Diners choose their appetizers and entrees from these tanks, assured that what they are eating is nothing but the freshest.

Equally important is preparation. The Leschi Lakecafe takes your fresh seafood and prepares it simply, usually grilling, pan frying or steaming. To this they add simple sauces that enhance but don't hide the taste of the fish.

Add a wonderful location on Lake Washington to a relaxed atmosphere and good service, and you have a great dining experience.

Leschi Lakecafe is located at 102 Lakeside Avenue, Seattle. Call 328-2233 for reservations.

CURRIED CHICKEN SALAD

A LA - Leschi Lake Cafe

1	**lb. poached chicken breasts** (cut into 1" by 1" cubes)
6	**oz. apples-equal ratio red & green** (diced - unpeeled)
6	**oz. seedless grapes** (preferably red flame-green seedless ok)
6	**oz. celery** (sliced into 1/4" pieces)
3	**oz. slivered almonds** (toasted)
1-1/2	**oz. black currants** (or substitute raisins)
1-1/2	**oz. green onions** (chopped)
1-1/2	**cups** *Curried Chutney Dressing* (recipe on next page)
	slivered almonds (garnish)
4	**lettuce leaves** (garnish)

1. Place all ingredients in bowl except garnishes and toss carefully so as not to bruise fruit.
2. Cover tightly and refrigerate several hours or overnight but no more than 12 hours.
3. Serve on lettuce leaf and garnish with almonds.

Serves: 4
Preparation: 20 minutes
Refrigeration: 6-12 hours

Excellent salad or main dish for a hot summer evening. Make enough - one husband ate the entire meal for four.

CURRIED CHUTNEY DRESSING

A LA - Leschi Lake Cafe

4	fl. oz. mayonnaise
4	fl. oz. sour cream
3	fl. oz. Sharwood's Peach Chutney*
1	T. curry powder
1	t. fresh ginger (peeled & finely minced)
1/2	t. salt
3	T. port vinaigrette**
1/8	t. Tabasco sauce

1. Place all ingredients in large bowl and mix with wire whisk until smooth.
2. Store refrigerated for 6 hours before using so that flavors can blend. Dressing keeps for one week.

Yield: 1-3/4 cups
Preparation: 10 minutes

*Sharwood's Chutney is available in your local grocery either in condiment or gourmet sections. Use another brand if this isn't available.
**You can make your own; just mix 2-1/2 tablespoons oil and 1 teaspoon wine vinegar.

A delicious dressing for the Curried Chicken Salad **recipe, previous page, or use your imagination for using it on other foods.**

161

BASE BUTTER

A LA - Leschi Lake Cafe

1	**lb. butter** (softened)
2	**T. parsley** (chopped)
1	**T. garlic** (chopped)
3	**T. lemon juice**
1/8	**t. cayenne**
1/8	**t. freshly ground black pepper**
1/2	**t. salt**

1. Place all ingredients in the work bowl of a food processor fitted with a steel blade or place in mixing bowl if blending by hand.
2. Turn motor on and let butter whip for 1-1/2 to 2 minutes. If necessary during mixing, turn off food processor to scrape down the sides. Take care to see that all ingredients are well-blended.
3. Store refrigerated until ready to use. Shelf life: 1 week.

Yield: 11 oz. (scant 1-1/2 cups)
Preparation: 5 minutes

This Base Butter can be used, as is, for all fish and vegetables. It is also an ingredient for the *Lime-Ginger Jalepeno Butter* next page. It is also a marvelous spread for hot garlic bread.

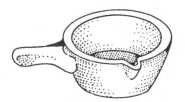

LIME-GINGER JALEPENO BUTTER

For Broiled Fish

A LA - Leschi Lake Cafe

1-1/2 **cups Base Butter** (softened-see recipe previous page)
1/4 **cup ginger** (finely minced)
1 **T. fresh jalepeno** (minced)
2 **T. lime juice** (freshly squeezed)

1. Place all ingredients in the work bowl of a food processor fitted with a steel blade or place in mixing bowl if blending by hand.
2. Turn motor on and let butter whip for 1-1/2 to 2 minutes. If necessary during mixing, turn off food processor to scrape down the sides. Take care to see that all ingredients are well-blended.
3. Store refrigerated until ready to use. Shelf life: 1 week

Yield: 1 lb.
Preparation: 5 minutes

Turn any fish or vegetable dish into a feast. Great on all tuna types, swordfish, sturgeon, shark and spearfish; and vegetables such as carrots, snow peas or cauliflower.

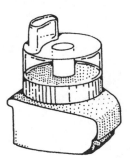

PRAWNS PICANTE

A LA - Leschi Lake Cafe

2	T. olive oil
1/4	cup red bell pepper (julienned 1/8" by 1")*
1/4	cup green bell pepper (julienned 1/8" by 1")*
1	T. fresh jalepeno pepper (halved, seeded and cut crosswise into 1/8" pieces)
1/4	cup red onion (sliced)
1-1/2	lbs. peeled Alaskan spot prawns**(tails off)
2	t. garlic (finely minced)
1/4	cup Gold Tequila
4	t. tomato puree
1/2	cup tomato (seeded, diced into 1/2" cubes)
3	T. green olives (sliced)
2	t. capers
3	T. lemon juice
2	t. fresh cilantro (chopped)-(Chinese parsley)

1. Have all ingredients ready.
2. Heat olive oil in large pan over medium heat.
3. Add peppers and onion. Saute 30 seconds until vegetables are soft.
4. Add shrimp; saute 1 minute. Add garlic.
5. Pour in Tequila and *flamber* (see Glossary).
6. Immediately add tomato puree, fresh tomato, olives, capers and lemon juice. Saute 1-2 minutes until prawns just done - pink, resilient, not hard. Remove from heat.

- continued -

7.   Add cilantro and toss. Spread out ingredients on hot
         serving platter and serve.

Serves: 4
Preparation: 20 minutes (add 20 minutes if you need to peel
prawns)

*See how to *julienne* vegetables in Glossary
**Alternative fish or shollfish aro: rockfish, cod, halibut or
scallops.

**A very beautiful dish - lovely color and marvelous taste. A
great idea for company. Try serving with sour dough
bread and butter.**

SMOKED SALMON, CREAM CHEESE & CUCUMBER SANDWICH

A LA - Leschi Lake Cafe

Salmon Cream Cheese Mousse

3	oz. **hard-smoked Sockeye Salmon** (boned and trimmed)
5	oz. **Philadelphia cream cheese** (softened)
1	t. **capers** (drained)
1	T. **grainy mustard**
1	T. **fresh lemon juice**
2	t. **creamy horseradish sauce**
2	t. **fresh dill weed** (chopped)

Sandwich

2	**slices honey wheat bread**
1	T. **mayonnaise**
8	**thin cucumber slices**
4	**thin red onion slices**
3	**tomato slices** (1/4" thick)
1	**green lettuce leaf**

1. Mix together all mousse ingredients. Blend well until creamy.
2. Lay the two slices of bread side by side on a work surface. Spread mayonnaise evenly on both slices.
3. Spread 1-1/2 oz. of mousse on each slice. Take care that the mousse is spread evenly and out to the very edges of the bread.
4. Layer sandwich, starting with the cucumber slices, followed by the onion, cucumbers and tomato slices.
7. Lay the lettuce leaf on top of the tomatoes, then top the sandwich with the other slice of bread.
8. Carefully cut the sandwich into quarters on the diagonal.

Serves: 1 sandwich
Mousse yield: enough for 3-4 sandwiches
Preparation: 10 minutes

Tasty combination!

167

Mamounia

RESTAURANT

Ever dream of getting away from it all to an exotic land? Seattleites are lucky; they just have to go to Mamounia for an evening meal.

This authentic Moroccan Restaurant serves you under tented ceilings while reclining on couches and leather cushions. Hand carved teak tables hold you meal and Oriental carpets decorate the walls.

In this exotic atmosphere, enjoy a meal consisting of Moroccan Salad, a flavorful dish of seasoned green peppers and tomatoes; followed by Chicken Pastilla; Brochettes; or Lamb and Onions. You will be transported away by the delicious aroma, fine food and great service.

Make your own exotic meal with these recipes from Mamounia and get away from it all!

Mamounia Moroccan Restaurant is located at 1556 Olive Way East, Seattle. Call 329-3886 for reservations.

MOROCCAN SALAD

A LA - Mamounia Moroccan Restaurant

3	ripe tomatoes
2	large green peppers
1/2	cup parsley (chopped)
1/4	t. cumin
1/8	cup vinegar
1/4	t. powdered coriander
1/2	cup olive oil
	salt and pepper (to taste)

1. Roast tomatoes and peppers over open flame, electric grill or under broiler. Turn vegetables until skin is black.
2. Drop in basin of cold water.
3. Remove blackened skins from tomatoes and green peppers. Remove seeds from peppers.
4. Cut and dice vegetables. Place in salad bowl.
5. Add remaining ingredients. Mix well.
6. Refrigerate 1-1/2 hours then serve.

Serves: 4
Preparation: 20 minutes
Refrigeration: 1-1/2 hours

Very refreshing. Chefs says this dish is eaten anytime during Moroccan meals. Can help you digest even the heartiest of meals.

PASTILLA

A LA - Mamounia Moroccan Restaurant

3	**lb. chicken with giblets** (cut in four parts)
1	**onion** (cut up)
1	**bunch parsley** (chopped)
1/4	**t. salt**
1/8	**t. pepper**
1/8	**t. ginger**
1/8	**t. coriander**
1	**cup oil**
3	**T. butter**
1	**pinch saffron**
5	**eggs** (beaten)
8-10	**sheets Fillo* dough** (cut in half) (thawed, kept covered with damp cloth)
6	**T. butter**
1	**cup almonds** (toasted) (crushed until fine)
2	**T. powdered sugar**
3	**T. cinnamon**

1. Place chicken and giblets, onion and parsley in large sauce pan.
2. Season with salt, pepper, ginger, coriander, oil, butter and saffron.
3. Add 4-1/2 cups water.
4. Cook for at least 1 hour or until chicken pulls easily from bones.
5. Remove; let cool. Save sauce.
6. Pull chicken meat from bones. Remove skin and shred meat into strips 1x2 inches. Set aside.
7. Let sauce cook over medium high heat until all water evaporates. You will have oil, butter, parsley, and onions remaining.
8. Cook eggs in this mixture. Stir until soft curds form. Set aside.

- continued -

172

Assemble Pastilla

9. Preheat oven 350º.
10. Cover bottom and sides of cast iron fry pan or other oven proof fry pan with light film of butter.
11. Lay 1 piece of Fillo dough on bottom and up sides of pan.
12. Using several more sheets of Fillo, completely cover sides of fry pan. Brush with butter between each sheet. Brush sides with butter.
13. Top Fillo with almonds, sugar and cinnamon.
14. Top with additional layer of Fillo. Brush with butter.
15. Place shredded chicken on top of Fillo.
16. Top with more Fillo, brush with butter.
17. Pour egg mixture on top of Fillo.
18. Using additional Fillo completely cover egg mixture. Brush with butter.
19. Gently fold all edges of Fillo down over top layer to completely enclose filling. Brush with butter.
20. Place fry pan in 350º oven for 5-10 minutes until top begins turning a golden brown.
21. Remove from oven and set over medium high heat for 5 minutes so that bottom is golden also.
22. Top fry pan with round serving platter. Flip pan over so that pastilla is on serving platter.
23. Dust top with powdered sugar and cinnamon.
24. Serve piping hot.

Serves: 8-10
Preparation: 2 hours-can be done in stages
Presentation: Mamounia notes that this is one of the most important steps. "One should use a large round plate made of elegant procelain". Enjoy!
*You'll find Fillo dough in frozen section of grocery store.

This dish is sure to be a hit at your next dinner party. Don't be detered by number of steps. It is very orderly and easy to assemble and you <u>will get raves</u>! It's delicious.

173

LAMB AND ONIONS

A LA - Mamounia Moroccan Restaurant

2	**lbs. boneless lamb shoulder** (cut in pieces)
3	**T. oil**
1/2	**T. salt**
1/2	**T. pepper**
1/2	**T. ginger**
1	**pinch saffron**
1/2	**t. coriander**
1	**lb. white onion** (sliced in thick rings)

1. Rinse meat under cold water.
2. Place in sauce pan with oil, salt, pepper, ginger, saffron, and coriander (do not skimp on spices)!
3. Barely cover with water.
4. Cook covered over medium heat for 3/4 of hour.
5. Add onions and cook for additional 3/4 hour.
6. Serve meat on platter, onions around side. Pour sauce from pan over all.

Serves: 4-5
Preparation: 1-3/4 hours

Try this for a great taste of Moroccan food.

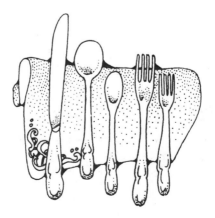

174

McCORMICK'S
FISH HOUSE & BAR

Seattle is known for the Seahawks, Sonics and partly cloudy days but restaurants such as McCormicks also put Seattle on the map for its seafood.

As you enter, the dark woodwork and pew-like benches lend solidity to the seriousness of eating well here. The antique bar and pictures punctuate the turn of the century mood.

A blackboard with one of the most extensive fresh fish menus, often includes such rarities as Shark and Swordfish prepared to tender perfection. The Clam Chowder is memorable and the ample wine list and attentive staff will make you feel you've escaped the 20th century for one warm intimate evening of dining where many a Seattleite flock only to find what they may have thought was a well kept secret haven is actually a well filled locale.

To insure an evening of delicious pleasure make reservations and enjoy.

McCormick's is located at 722 4th Avenue, Seattle. Call 682-3900 for reservations .

GULF PRAWNS WITH BRANDY AND CREAM

A LA - McCormick's Fish House And Bar

1/2	**cup butter** (clarified*)
16	**large mushrooms** (quartered)
24-28	**large prawns** (peeled and deveined)
2/3	**cup brandy**
3	**t. grain mustard**
2/3	**cup whipping cream**
1	**T. minced green onion**
2	**cups rice** (cooked)

1. Heat butter; add mushrooms; saute for 1 minute.
2. Add prawns; saute for additional minute.
3. Deglaze** pan with brandy; add mustard and saute for 30 seconds.
4. Add cream and onions. Cook until reduced by half and sauce thickens.
5. Serve immediately over rice.

Serves: 4
Preparation: 15 minutes

*See Clarified in Glossary
**See *Deglaze* in Glossary

Delicious-a favorite!

YELLOW-FIN TUNA WITH SOY MADEIRA SAUCE

A LA - McCormick's Fish House And Bar

1	**lb. uncooked yellow-fin tuna** (cut in 4 oz. portions)*
1/2	**cup flour**
	oil
3/4	**cup Madeira wine**
1	**T. soy sauce**
1	**orange**
3/4	**cup whipping cream**
1/4	**lb. butter**
2	**cups white rice** (cooked)

1. Preheat oven to 350º.
2. Lightly flour tuna; dust off excess.
3. Pan-fry in oil until brown on both sides.
4. Place in oven to bake until done, about 5 minutes.
5. In sauce pan, combine Madeira wine, soy sauce and juice from orange.
6. Heat to boiling. Add cream and reduce for one minute.
7. Add butter, a little at a time, stirring constantly.
8. Heat until will combined and thickened, but do not boil.
9. Serve tuna over rice, topped with sauce.

Serves: 4
Preparation: 20 minutes

*The most commonly available fresh tuna at your local market.

A wonderful dish. Sauce is great. A must for anyone who only thinks tuna comes in a can! Sauce would be great over chicken too.

BAY SCALLOPS CEVICHE

A LA - McCormick's Fish House And Bar

Ceviche

1-1/2	**oz. bay scallops** (raw-shelled)
10	**limes**
2	**lemons**
1/4	**cup black olives** (chopped)
1/4	**cup green olives** (sliced)
1/4	**cup green pepper** (diced)
1/4	**cup red pepper** (diced)
1/4	**cup onion** (sliced)
2	**jalepeno peppers** (diced)
2	**T. fresh cilantro** (Chinese Parsley) (chopped)

lettuce (garnish)
parsley sprigs (garnish)
lemon slices (garnish)
crackers or sourdough bread (garnish)

Ceviche

1. Place scallops in glass bowl.
2. Add juice from limes and lemons and let set for at least 1 hour.
3. Combine all vegetables with scallops.
4. Refrigerate for at least 4 hours to marinate.

5. To serve: drain juice; arrange *ceviche* on lettuce; garnish with parsley and lemon slices.
6. Serve as appetizer with crackers or bread.

Serves: 4-6
Preparation: 10 minutes
Refrigeration: 4 hours

A refreshing light appetizer.

178

MIKADO FISH & TEMPURA CO.

Another Mikado success story can be found near the waterfront, featuring fresh fish, Tempura Prawns, and Teriyaki Beef and Chicken, as well as other tasty Japanese specialties.

The main attraction here is the wonderful Sushi and Sake bar. Chef Jin Sato orchestrates the art of cutting only the freshest fish to your delight while offering the largest Sake selection in Seattle.

It often takes up to 10 years to be considered a truly accomplished Sushi Chef and as you watch the skillful speed and accuracy with which the fish becomes a work of art, you will appreciate this.

Sushi-bar eating is an experience that promotes a certain casual friendliness. However, if you haven't time for the social event, there's also a Sushi take-out service and catering available.

Mikado is located at 83 Spring Street at Waterfront Place, Seattle. Reservations for special events only, 622-0659.

179

MISO SOUP

A LA - Mikado Fish and Tempura Co.

4   **cups hondashi*** (fish stock chicken broth or beef bouillion)
1/4   **cup miso paste** (fermented soy bean paste)
2   **t. saki** or sherry
1   **cup tofu** (cut in 1" squares)
2   **green onions** (chopped)
       wakame (dried seaweed found in Oriental markets) (optional)

1.   Combine broth, miso paste and saki over medium high heat.
2.   Heat to hot temperature but do not boil.
3.   Place tofu cubes, green onions and wakame in individual bowls. Pour hot broth over and serve.

Serves: 4-6
Preparation: 10 minutes

*Buy hondashi in powdered form in Oriental market. Mix 4 t. with 4 cups water.

Traditional 1st course for Japanese dinners. Also good as a snack.

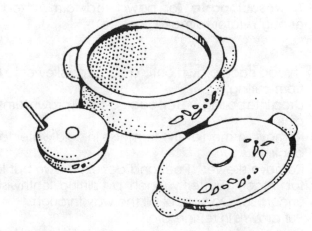

NIGIRI SUSHI
Prawn Sushi

A LA - Mikado Fish and Tempura Co.

12	**large raw prawns** (unshelled)
12	**bamboo skewers**
1/3	**cup rice vinegar**
1	**t. sugar**
1	**t. salt**
2	**cups short grain rice** (cooked and barely cooled to body temperature)
1/2	**cup water**
1/2	**cup rice vinegar**
1	**T. wasabi paste** (or powdered form mixed with enough water to make a paste)

1. Thread each prawn onto a bamboo skewer to keep from curling.
2. Drop into boiling water; cook just until prawn turns light pink.
3. Remove immediately. Immerse in cold water to stop cooking
4. Remove skewer. Peel and devein prawn but leave tail intact. Butterfly each by slitting lenthwise on underside. Do not cut all the way through.
5. Put prawns in refrigerator.
6. Combine rice vinegar, sugar and salt in pan. Heat just until warm to touch. Do not boil.
7. Add to rice; stir and fan until cooled to body temperature.
8. Combine water and rice vinegar.
9. Wet hands in vinegar water.

- continued -

182

10.   Dab small amount of wasabi in slit side of prawn.
11.   Take 1 tablespoon rice mixture and place in slit side of prawn.
12.   Lay rice side down on serving platter until all are made.
13.   Serve with additional wasabi if desired.

Serves: 6
Preparation: 25 minutes

Chef says to always keep rice at body temperature when handling.

Delicious way to enjoy sushi. Have a sushi party for your next event. Use seasoned rice with raw tuna, red snapper, smelt and goeduck! Certain fish can not be eaten raw; steam or boil octopus, salmon, eel or cod.

TEMPURA SAUCE

A LA - Mikado Fish and Tempura Co.

4   **cups hondashi, fish stock or water**
1   **cup soy sauce**
1/4   **cup sugar**
1/4   **cup saki**
2   **T. grated fresh ginger** (or to taste)

1.   Combine water (or hondashi) soy and sugar.
2.   Bring to boil.
3.   Add saki and ginger to your taste.
4.   Serve warm as dipping sauce for tempura.

Serves: 4-6
Preparation: 10 minutes

Traditional light sauce for tempura. Try with both chicken and vegetables. Would be good with Duke's Szechuan Chicken or Duke's Tempura.

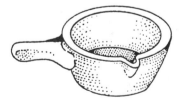

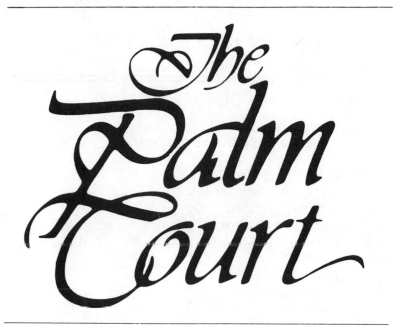

The Palm Court is renowned throughout the Northwest region for its fine dining. Serving quality Northwest and regional dishes for lunch and dinner, popular menu items include the Filet Mignon with Blueberry Sauce and Coho Fillets with Chardonnay Sauce. An extensive Northwest wine list complements the menu.

A feeling of elegant dining permeates the atmosphere of The Palm Court. Located off the lobby of The Westin Hotel, its design features four glass pavilions, particularly impressive at night. Furnishings include crystal chandeliers, brocade fabrics, and custom designed china and crystal. An imported orchid graces each table.

An annual award winner of the prestigious Travel Holiday Award since it opened in October of 1981, The Palm Court is acclaimed for its quality of food, elegant atmosphere and excellent service.

The Palm Court is located in The Westin Hotel at 1900 Fifth Avenue, Seattle. Call 728-1000 for reservations.

DUNGENESS CRAB CAKES
(Begin at least 1 hour ahead)

A LA - The Palm Court

1	**egg** (beaten)
1-1/2	**cups soft white bread crumbs**
2	**T. butter**
1/2	**cup onion** (minced)
1/2	**cup green pepper** (diced)
2	**T. celery** (minced)
1	**lb. flaked crabmeat**
1/2	**t. salt**
1/4	**t. thyme**
	pinch of cayenne
2	**T. mayonnaise**
1	**T. parsley** (chopped)
1	**cup oil**
	tartar sauce

1. Combine egg and bread crumbs in medium bowl.
2. Melt butter over medium heat. Add onion and green pepper. Cook until lightly browned, about 3-5 minutes.
3. Add celery.
4. Combine onion, pepper, celery mix with crabmeat, salt, thyme and cayenne.
5. Mix together and add to egg mix.
6. Stir in mayonnaise and parsley.
7. Chill mix for 1 hour.
8. Form into small cakes.
9. Heat oil in deep pan. Fry cakes until golden brown; 5-6 minutes.
10. Drain on absorbent paper.
11. Serve with tartar sauce.

Serves: 4
Preparation: 20 minutes

**An _easy_ first course or light dinner fare!
Delicious!**

186

TARTARE OF FRESH TUNA WITH OLIVE OIL AND CHIVES

A LA - The Palm Court

6	oz. very fresh raw tuna (diced)
3	T. olive oil
1	egg yolk
1	lemon
1	t. fresh dill (chopped)
1	t. fresh chives (chopped)
1	t. Dijon mustard
2	anchovies (mashed)
1	T. Bermuda onion (minced)
1	t. capers (minced)
	salt and pepper (to taste)
	radicchio leaves (red tipped green leaf lettuce)
	red pepper (thinly sliced)
2	t. sevruga Caviar (optional)
	pumpernickle bread or toast points (remove crust from toast and cut into 4 triangles)

1. Place tuna in bowl.
2. Combine remaining ingredients (excep caviar,t red pepper strips and toast).
3. Fold into diced tuna. Taste to correct seasoning. Add salt and pepper to your taste if necessary.
4. Chill.
5. To serve, spoon into radicchio leaves; garnish with red pepper slices. Put 1 teaspoon of caviar on top of each serving (optional) and serve with toast or pumpernickle.

Serves: 2
Preparation: 5 minutes

Very fresh tuna is the secret of this recipe's success. Dressing would also be great over canned tuna or any fish.

187

STEAMED FILLET of COHO with SCALLOPS and CHARDONNAY SAUCE

A LA - The Palm Court

Chardonnay Sauce
2	**T. butter** (clarified)
2	**T. shallot onions** (diced)
1/2	**cup Chardonnay** or white wine
3/4	**cup whipping cream**
	salt and white pepper

4	**(4-6 oz.) Coho fillets**
1/2	**celery stalk** (julienned)**
1/2	**carrot** (julienned)**
1/2	**leek** white part
12	**large scallops** (poached)
1	**t. salmon caviar**
1	**t. black caviar**
1	**t. pink caviar**
1	**t. chives** (minced)

Chardonnay Sauce
1. Heat butter in sauce pan. Add shallots; saute for 1 minute. Do not brown.
2. Add wine; cook and reduce until liquid is evaporated.
3. Pour in cream; reduce by one third by cooking.
4. Season to taste with salt and pepper. Set aside and keep warm.

- continued -

188

5. Flatten Coho fillets gently with mallet or plate.
6. Lay julienned vegetables across each fillet.
7. Roll fillets up. Make slash halfway through.
8. Steam over boiling water until done, 10-15 minutes.
9. Place rolled fish on plate and pour sauce around it.
10. Place 3 poached scallops in front of each fish roll. Decorate each with a different kind of caviar on top. Garnish fish with chives.

Serves: 4
Preparation: 30 minutes

*See *Clarified* in Glossary
**See *Julienne* in Glossary

Colorful dish. Yummy light sauce.

SAUTEED FILET MIGNON and KIWI FRUIT with BLUEBERRY SAUCE

A LA - The Palm Court

2	**lbs. fresh or frozen blueberries**
1/4	**cup honey**
1/4	**cup red wine**
1/2	**cup port wine**
	salt and pepper (to taste)
1	**cup brown sauce** (buy packaged gravy sauce)
4	**7 oz. center cut filet mignons**
	salt and pepper (to taste)
	rosemary (to taste)
2	**whole kiwis** (peeled and sliced)
16-20	**whole blueberries**

1. Combine blueberries, honey and red wine in large sauce pan. Bring to boil.
2. Remove from heat and strain berries through a fine mesh strainer.
3. Return juice to pan and bring to a boil again; add port wine. Do not let boil too much or flavor is lost.
4. Season to taste with salt and pepper.
5. Add brown sauce and keep warm.
6. Season filets with salt, pepper and rosemary.
7. Pan fry over moderate heat until done to desired degree, 2-3 minutes each side for medium.
8. Coat each plate with 1/4 cup sauce, top with filet and 3-4 kiwi slices.
9. Serve additional sauce on side with whole berries.

Serves: 4
Preparation: 15 minutes

A very colorful entree with a taste to match. Easy to do and very impressive.

190

POOR ITALIAN CAFE

As Christopher Morley once said, "No one is ever lonely eating spaghetti, it requires too much attention." And attention is what the Poor Italian Cafe gives to its patrons, and attracts for its excellent food.

The Poor Italian Cafe is located just off Second Avenue on Virginia. Owner Gregory Pesce or one of his six Italian sisters-in-law is likely to give you a warm welcome to their delightful family owned and operated eating establishment.

A lovely antique bar, stained glass chandeliers from Italy and a wine cask, which Gregory made by hand while earning his credentials at the North Beach Restaurant in San Francisco, add sparkle and interest to the decor.

Like his mentors before him, Gregory succeeds in offering, as the main attraction, good food at good prices. A menu "rich with the taste of Italy" beckons you with such wonders as Fettuccine Carbonara, Gnocchi, Calamari Livornese, Spaghetti Ricardo and Veal Milanese.

The pasta, always fresh and homemade, comes with nine sauce varieties. The light pesto, a regional specialty of Liguria (The Italian Riviera), is a favorite. Chef Richard offers up to six daily specials and will even whip up orders to go.

Visit The Poor Italian and experience the warmth and goodness that always come from genuine Italian cuisine, zestfully prepared with a pinch of love and dedication.

The Poor Italian is located at 2000 Second Avenue, Seattle. Call 441-4313 for reservations.

VEAL MILANESE

A LA - Poor Italian Cafe

1	**lb. veal cutlets** (cut into medallions)
1/2	**cup flour**
4	**eggs** (beaten)
1	**cup dry bread crumbs**
1/2	**pinch of basil**
1/2	**pinch of oregano**
	salt and pepper (to taste)
1	**T. parsley**
1	**T. parmesan cheese**
1/4	**cup olive oil**
2	**cloves garlic** (minced)
	juice of 2 lemons
1	**T. parmesan cheese**
1	**T. romano cheese**
1	**T. fresh parsley** (chopped)

1. Pound cutlets until tender.
2. Dust with flour; shake off excess.
3. Dip medallions into egg wash, then into bread crumbs mixed with basil, oregano, salt, pepper, parsley and parmesan cheese.
4. Heat olive oil and garlic. Saute medallions over medium high heat until lightly browned, approximately 45 seconds each side.
5. Sprinkle with juice from lemons.
6. Remove from pan; dust with cheeses and parsley and serve.

Serves: 4
Preparation: 10 minutes

A wonderful flavor combination and so easy! Great with pasta and vegetables.

VEAL OR CHICKEN MARSALA

A LA - Poor Italian Cafe

1	**lb. veal cutlets** (or chicken if you prefer)
1/2	**cup flour**
2	**T. butter**
1/2	**cup mushrooms** (sliced)
1/2	**cup onions** (chopped)
1/2	**cup pimentoes** (sliced)
1	**T. fresh parsley** (chopped)
1	**l. busll**
	salt and pepper (to taste)
1/2	**cup sweet Marsala wine**

1. Pound cutlets until well tenderized.
2. Dust with flour and cut into small medallions or thin fillets.
3. Melt butter in saute pan over high heat. Add cutlets, mushrooms, onions, pimentoes, parsley, basil and salt and pepper.
4. Cook until onions are transparent, 5-6 minutes.
5. Add Marsala. Saute until thick sauce forms, about 6 minutes.
6. Serve immediately!

Serves: 4
Preparation: 15 minutes

This recipe is great with chicken or veal! Serve with spaghetti and salad for a quick, easy meal.

CHICKEN PICCATA

A LA - Poor Italian Cafe

4	(7 oz.) boneless, skinless chicken breasts
1/2	cup flour
1	cup butter
1	cup mushrooms (sliced)
	juice of 2 lemons
1	cup white wine
1	T. capers
1	T. parsley (chopped)
4	lemon slices
4	parsley sprigs

1. Pound chicken breasts until thin.
2. Flour breasts and cut into strips.
3. Melt butter in heavy frying pan.
4. Saute breasts until lightly browned on both sides and flour is dissolved, approximately 3-4 minutes.
5. Add mushrooms, lemon juice, white wine and capers.
6. Cook until ingredients are combined and sauce thickens, 7-8 minutes.
7. Add parsley and serve immediately, garnished with lemon slices and parsley sprigs.

Serves: 4
Preparation: 20 minutes

A quick delicious entree. Perfect for easy entertaining. Equally good with veal.

PARSLEY

Prego, located high in the Stouffer Madison Hotel, is an elegant roof-top restaurant that is a favorite destination for spectators.

With all of Seattle as a spectacular back drop and furnishings of understated elegance, Prego is the perfect place to enjoy a fine evening meal featuring Northern Italian cuisine.

Carefully prepared for your enjoyment, the menu features sauces, grilled meats and a wide selection of seafood entrees all lighter than the Mediterranean counterpart one usually thinks of as Italian cuisine.

To capture this elegant mood at your dinner table, try the Grilled Chicken Breast with Shallots or Salmon Filet on Braised Lettuce with Herb Sauce, done to perfection. The chefs at Prego have graciously shared their recipes with us.

Prego is located at 515 Madison Street, Seattle. Call 583-0300 for reservations.

CANNELONI of DUNGENESS CRAB, SALMON MOUSSE and SPINACH

A LA - Prego

12	**canneloni squares** (fresh) (use fresh lazagne sheets cut in squares or packaged dry manicotti pasta shells)
1/8	**lb. salmon**
1	**egg white**
1/2	**cup whipping cream**
1/4	**lb. dungeness crab**
1	**cup spinach leaves** (washed and torn)
	salt and pepper
1/2	**cup white wine**
1/2	**cup clam juice** or fish stock*
1/2	**cup onion** (finely diced)
1	**T. olive oil**
1	**bay leaf**
1	**sprig thyme** (pinch of dry)
1	**lb. tomatoes** (diced)
2	**leaves fresh basil** (pinch of dry)
1	**clove garlic** (minced)
1	**T. chives**

1. Cook canneloni in boiling, salted water for 2 minutes. Immediately plunge into cold water and spread flat. (If you use packaged manicotti shells, cook according to package directions).
2. In processor combine salmon and egg white. Slowly add whipping cream, 1 tablespoonful at a time.
3. Fold in crab and spinach (1 second in processor). Season to taste with salt and pepper.
4. Spoon mousse in center of canneloni.
5. Roll into cylinder shape. Place in greased shallow baking pan.
6. Add white wine and fish stock.
7. Bake 15-20 minutes until mousse is cooked.

- continued -

8   Meanwhile, slowly cook onion in olive oil in saute pan
        with bay leaf and thyme. Do not brown.
9.   Add tomatoes. Cook until sauce thickens.
10.   Season with basil, garlic and chives. Heat until hot.
11.   Place canneloni on plates; cover with sauce and
        serve.

Serves: 4-6
Preparation: 45 minutes

*Clam juice comes canned in supermarkets, or you can use
fish stock recipe in Glossary.

**A light dish-perfect with green salad and sourdough
bread.**

FILLETS OF SALMON ON BRAISED LETTUCE WITH HERB SAUCE

A LA - Prego

1/4	**cup shallot onions** (chopped)
1/4	**cup butter**
1/2	**cup white wine**
1	**pint whipping cream**
3/4	**lb. butter**
1	**bunch chives** (chopped)
1/4	**cup butter**
4	**cloves garlic** (mashed)
2	**heads red leaf lettuce** (washed; coarsely chopped)
4	**6 oz. fillets of King Salmon**
	8 oz. fish stock or clam juice*
4	**potatoes** (boiled) or rice (optional)

1. Cook shallots, 1/4 cup butter and wine in a sauce pan until wine has evaporated, approximately 4-5 minutes. Do not brown butter.
2. Add cream and cook over medium heat until reduced by half. (This takes about 10 minutes).
3. Reduce heat to warm and slowly whisk in 3/4 lb. butter in 1 tablespoon amounts until a creamy butter sauce forms.
4. Add chives and hold over barely warm heat. Do not boil or sauce will separate.
5. Heat 1/4 cup butter and garlic cloves over medium high heat. Add red lettuce and saute until wilted. Keep warm.

- continued -

6. In flat frying pan or saute pan poach fillets in fish stock until done. Do not over cook or fish will fall apart.
7. To serve, place lettuce on serving platter; top with fish fillets and strain herb sauce over fillets. Serve with plain boiled potato or rice.

Serves: 4
Preparation: 30 minutes

*Available in your local grocery store.

This is the most delicious tasting dish. Test kitchen found it moist and flavorful. It is also a very pleasing presentation. A Must for a special meal.

CHIVES

SUPREME OF CHICKEN WITH BRAISED SHALLOTS

A LA - Prego

1	**cup shallots** (sliced)
1	**T. butter** (more if needed)
2	**t. vinegar**
1/2	**cup white wine**
1	**qt. veal** or chicken stock
4	**chicken breasts** (6 oz. each)
4	**sprigs of fresh thyme**

1. Cook shallots slowly in the butter until transparent.
2. Add vinegar and white wine and allow to reduce completely by cooking until all liquid is evaporated.
3. Add veal stock and allow to cook over high heat until reduced to 1 cup of sauce (about 15 minutes).
4. Saute or grill chicken breasts using a little fresh thyme to season. Do not overcook chicken.
5. To serve, pour sauce on plate. Slice the chicken breast and place on top of the sauce. Garnish with small vegetables and serve with potato or rice.

Serves: 4
Preparation: 20 minutes

A tasty, light way to prepare chicken. Fast and Easy.

THYME

When the conversation turns to Seattle, the inevitable question is, "Have you been to Ray's?" A resounding "Yes!", serves to bind seafood lovers everywhere, while giving Ray's international recognition.

The reason, of course, is the consistently excellent cuisine accompanying one of the best views of Shilshole Bay and of dramatic Northwest sunsets.

Though a mishap temporarily closed Ray's Boathouse, the original cozy boathouse decor is being rebuilt to give you, once again, the Ray's you've known and loved. An unscathed Ray's will be ready to serve you by Spring, 1988.

In the First Interstate Center, is the elegant Ray's Downtown, which is a sophisticated version of the original, offering the same fabulous King Crab, Poached Salmon with Mustards, Tarragon and Cream and every imaginable fresh seafood dish.

Ray's Boathouse is located at 6049 Seaview Avenue N.W.; call 789-3770. The downtown location is at 999 Third Avenue, First Interstate Center; call 623-7999.

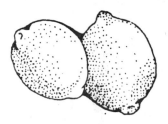

GARLIC

SAUTEED SPOT SHRIMP IN OLIVE OIL

A LA - Ray's

1	**lb. spot shrimp** (30-40 per lb. size) **in shell**
3	**oz. olive oil**
3	**cloves garlic** (chopped)
1	**t. salt**
1/2	**lemon** (juiced)
	parsley (chopped for garnish)

1. Heat olive oil in large skillet with garlic.
2. Toss in shrimp and saute for about 30 seconds.
3. Add lemon juice and salt and saute until done, about 3 minutes.
4. Garnish with chopped parsley.

Serves: 4 as appetizer
Preparation: 5 minutes

This specialty of Chef Wayne Ludvigson is so easy and so good.

POACHED SALMON

A LA - Ray's

1	qt. water
1	qt. fish stock or clam juice*
1	cup chablis wine
3	bay leaves
3	whole peppercorns
1/2	bunch parsley
1	small pinch thyme
1/2	lemon, juice only
3	lbs. salmon fillets *or* 6 (8 oz.) small fillets

1. Combine all ingredients, except salmon, in pot large enough to hold fillets later.
2. Bring to a rolling boil for 15 minutes.
3. Strain. Discard vegetables.
4. Return liquid to heat and keep just under a boil.
5. Place rack on bottom of pot. Place fillet on top, completely submerged.
6. Poach salmon until done, approximately 10 minutes for each inch of fillet thickness - not length.
7. Remove; serve warm or cold.
8. Save liquid for fish stock or soup base at future date.

Serves: 4-6
Preparation: 25 minutes

*Clam juice is available in grocery canned section. If you prefer-there's a fish stock recipe in the Glossary.

This is the best way to poach salmon. Fillet is flavorful but not over cooked.

204

POACHED SALMON WITH MUSTARD, TARRAGON & CREAM

A LA - Ray's

2-1/4	cups fish stock
3/4	cup chablis wine
1	T. shallot onions (chopped)
1	cup whipping cream
1-3	T. stone ground Dijon mustard
1-3	T. stone ground tarragon mustard**
3	T. cold butter
6	(8oz.) fillets (poached Salmon - hot*)

1. In large sauce pan, combine fish stock, wine and shallots.
2. Over high heat, cook until reduced to one fourth original amount. Mixture will turn golden brown and form large bubbles, about 5-8 minutes.
3. Reduce heat to medium and add cream and reduce by one half by cooking. Mixture should be thick enough to coat a wooden spoon. This should take around 10 minutes.
4. Add equal amounts of the mustards, according to your taste (from 1-3 tablespoons each).
5. Heat mixture to simmer and whisk in cold butter, bit by bit, until rich and creamy.
6. Spoon sauce over hot fillets and serve.

Serves: 6
Preparation: 20-25 minutes

*Use basic Poached Salmon recipe previous page, to poach fillets.
**Tarragon mustard is readily available in most supermarkets. If you cannot find, use all Dijon mustard with a pinch of tarragon herb.

A perfect complement to our Northwest favorite.

205

LEMON MOUSSE

A LA - Ray's

6	T. butter
3	eggs
2/3	cup sugar
1/2	cup fresh squeezed lemon juice (1-1/2 lemons)
1-1/2	cups whipping cream (chilled)
	zest of 1 lemon (grated peelings)

1. Melt butter in double boiler over simmering water.
2. Beat eggs and sugar in bowl until light and foamy.
3. Add melted butter and lemon juice.
4. Return mixture to double boiler.
5. Beat constantly with whip until mixture becomes a custard (5 minutes over medium-low heat). *Do not over-cook or eggs will scramble.*
6. Remove from heat and chill.
7. Whip cream until stiff.
8. Fold whipped cream and chilled custard together. Fold in lemon zest.
9. Pour into 6 individual serving glasses. Chill several hours in refrigerator until ready to serve.

Serves: 6
Preparation: 25 minutes
Refrigeration: 3 hours or more

Light, lemony and rich. Very Good!

206

RISTORANTE

One of the first genuine pearls in a strand of Northern Italian restaurants to grace the Northwest, Ristorante Settebello shines in serving wonderful foods at cultured prices.

Imported cheeses, olive oils, and vinegars enhance the flavors of the rich Northwest cornucopia. Owner Luciano Bardinelli's imaginative daily specials attract crowds for lunch a la Milano, which includes three courses, fixed prices and no menu. Dinner is hard to resist with the many clever creations from the market's daily bounty.

Ristorante Settebello which means "Beautiful Seven" in Italian makes me think of seven things I love here: the veal, fresh pastas, the freshest fish, the beef salad, the delicious gelati, the excellent wine and the cappuccino.

Come enjoy lunch or dinner and you'll be certain to return again and again to this sunny sky-lit spot for the variety and for the authentic Northern Italian flavors.

Ristorante Settebello is located at 1525 E. Olive Way, Seattle. Call 323-7772 for reservations.

CAPINATA
Eggplant Antipasto

A LA - Ristorante Settebello

1	**lb. eggplant** (about 2 small) (peeled and cut into small cubes)
1	**onion** (sliced)
	olive oil
2	**medium tomatoes** (put in food processor 3 seconds)
1/2	**cup celery** (finely diced)
1/2	**cup pitted black olives** (small riviera type)
2	**T. capers**
2	**T. virgin olive oil**
1/4	**cup white vinegar**
1	**t. sugar.**
2	**leaves, fresh basil** (or 1/2 t. of dry)

1. Sprinkle salt on diced eggplant and let sit for 1 hour so that bitter flavor is gone.
2. Saute onion in a little oil until golden color. Add tomatoes, celery, olives and capers.
3. Cook for about 20 minutes. Set aside.
4. In another pan, saute eggplant in 2 tablespoons oil until golden colored. Drain eggplant and add to tomato mixture, mix well.
5. Add vinegar and sugar. Cook on low heat until vinegar has evaporated.
6. Add fresh basil and remove from heat. Serve cold as antipasto or warm as a vegetable dish.

Serves: 4
Preparation: 35 minutes
Marinate: 1 hour

Colorful and refreshing antipasto.

WHITE BEAN SALAD

(Soak beans overnight)

A LA - Ristorante Settebello

1/2	**lb. dry cannellini** (white beans)
1/4	**onion** (finely chopped)
1/2	**cup parsley** (freshly chopped)
4	**t. virgin olive oil**
1	**t. red wine vinegar**
	salt and pepper (to taste)

1. Put beans in pot with cold water and let soak overnight.
2. Drain beans. Wash them. Put in pot with cold water and bring to a boil. Turn heat down, cover and simmer for 1-1/2 to 2 hours, or according to package directions, until done.
3. Drain beans and cool them.
4. Add onion parsley, oil and vinegar mixed together (add more if necessary). Season well with salt and pepper to taste.
5. Refrigerate until ready to serve.

Preparation: 5 minutes
Cooking: 2 hours
Soaking: 6 hours or overnight

Good luncheon side dish.

Saleh al Lago

Although Saleh Judeh studied medicine in Italy, it is his study and mastery of Italian food that draws us to his lovely restaurant.

Not only is the decor sophisticated in its soft pastel blues and apricots, but the cuisine invites the venturesome to taste the wonderfully presented, carefully perpared Central Italian fare; indluding Involtini Di Vitello, Gnocchi with Spinach and the Roman-style Saltimbocca with Prosciutto, Artichokes and Basil.

There is also a cozy cafe section next to the windows, perfect for a late-night snack or dessert, a drink or an espresso. Saleh al Lago provides an excellent combination of elegance and ease, with wonderful service to equal one great restaurant.

Saleh al Lago is located at 6804 E. Green Lake Way N., Seattle. Call 522-7943 for reservations. (Closed Sundays.)

HUMMOS
Sesame-Garbanzo Sauce

A LA - Saleh al Lago

1	**(8 oz.) can garbanzo beans**
1/2	**cup fresh lemon juice**
1/4	**cup water**
3	**cloves garlic**
1/2	**cup sesame tahini** (this is a sesame paste found in Oriental stores, health food stores and many supermarkets.
1	**t. salt**

1. Place garbanzo beans in food processor and puree.
2. Add ingredients that follow and blend in consecutive order. Blend until smooth.
3. Taste for seasonings. Add more lemon juice and salt if desired.
4. Use with *Tortellini* recipe next page.

Yield: 2 cups
Preparation: 5 minutes

Enjoy this delicious dip with vegetables, pita bread or chips or use as part of Tortellini recipe next page.

TORTELLINI MEDIO ORIENTALE

A LA - Saleh al Lago

3/4	**cup** *Hummos* (see recipe on preceding page)
3/4	**cup chicken stock**
1/2	**cup olive oil** (or more if needed)
	salt and pepper (to taste)
1	**lb. fresh tortellini, cooked** (preferably stuffed with chicken).
1	**cup fresh tomatoes** (diced)
2	**T. fresh parsley** (chopped)

1. Warm *Hummos* over low heat in saute pan and slowly stir in chicken stock and olive oil, stirring constantly to blend.
2. Add salt and pepper to suit your tastes.
3. Toss with cooked tortellini and garnish with tomatoes and parsley.

Serves: 4
Preparation: 12 minutes

Tasty dish.

MUSSELS WITH TOMATO SAUCE
Cozze Umbro

A LA - Saleh al Lago

1	T. olive oil
1/2	t. garlic (chopped)
	pinch of hot red pepper (crushed)
2	dozen Penn Cove mussels* or other mussels
1/4	cup dry white wine
1/2	cup chicken stock
1/4	cup tomato sauce (fresh cooked or tomato juice will do)
1/2	lemon (juiced)
	salt and pepper (to taste)
	parsley (freshly chopped)

1. In large skillet, heat olive oil and add garlic and hot pepper.
2. Add mussels and toss over medium heat for 1 minute.
3. Add wine and cook until liquid is reduced in half.
4. Add stock, tomato sauce, lemon juice and salt and pepper.
5. Continue to cook 2-3 minutes or until mussels are open. Sprinkle with parsley and serve in warm bowls.

Serves: 4 as appetizer
Preparation: 10 minutes

*Penn Cove mussels are the "elite" of mussels from the Olympic Peninsula.

Cooked just right in a tasty tomato sauce.

LINGUINE WITH ROASTED PEPPERS

A LA - Saleh al Lago

1	red bell pepper
1	yellow bell pepper
3	cloves garlic
1/2	cup olive oil
1/4	cup chicken stock (optional)
1	t. red wine vinegar
	salt and peper (to taste)
1/2	lb. fresh linguine noodles (cooked)
1	T. butter
1	T. parsley (freshly chopped)
2	T. mixed, grated parmesan and pecorino cheese (mixed together) (you may substitute romano for pecorino)

1. Roast peppers over open flame or under broiler until they are completely blackened. When cool, remove skin and seeds.
2. Puree top 6 ingredients in blender until smooth. Warm this puree in skillet and add salt and pepper to taste.
3. Toss with linguine and butter.
4. Garnish with parsley and grated mixed cheese.

Serves: 2
Preparation: 10 minutes

Exciting new taste for pasta.

215

SALMON IN PHYLLO WITH MONTRACHET SAUCE

A LA - Saleh al Lago

4	**(7 oz.) King Salmon Filets**
6	**leaves phyllo pastry - room temperature** (available in frozen food section)
4	**t. pesto sauce** (buy package variety)
2	**oz. peanut oil or other cooking oil** (or more if necessary)

Montrachet Sauce

2	**t. shallot onions** (chopped)
1/2	**lb. montrachet cheese, shredded** (available in most large supermarkets or use any goat cheese)
1/4	**cup dry white wine**
4	**T. butter**
4	**T. stock** (more or less to thin sauce)
1/2	**t. red wine vinegar**
1/2	**t. Fines Herbs** (find in spice section) or a mixture of fresh herbs

1. Preheat oven to 350º. Remove any remaining bones from filets.
2. Cut stack of phyllo leaves in half and then make 4 stacks of 3 leaves each.
3. Spread each filet with 1 teaspoon pesto and place on stack of phyllo to the right of center. Fold right side of pastry over salmon; then top and bottom over that. Then fold covered salmon to the left until you've encased it in a pastry envelope. (The idea of all this is to encase salmon in an envelope of pastry so that all of it is covered and sealed).

- continued -

216

4. In large skillet, warm oil over medium heat. Brown both sides of pastry just until golden.

5. Transfer to baking sheet and bake in 350º oven for 3-5 minutes until salmon is just cooked through. Don't overbake!

Montrachet Sauce

6. Over medium high heat, saute shallots in white wine until wine is reduced by half.

7. Add vinegar and over low heat slowly stir in butter until melted.

8. Fold in shredded Montrachet cheese and stir until melted.

9. Drizzle stock in slowly and stir until sauce coats spoon.

10. Add herbs and stir.

11. Pour sauce over salmon pastries and serve immediately. Chefs suggests you garnish them with sun-dried tomatoes (optional).

Serves: 4
Preparation: 20 minutes

Very impressive, very good and oh so easy!

Salty's

Salty's

For that purely Northwest, pleasureable feeling of watching sunsets over Puget Sound, strolling the beach, and observing fisherman on the pier, head for Salty's at Redondo. Here, you'll enjoy the finest waterfront dining in a casual, relaxed, yet up-scale atmosphere. The service is professional, but always friendly, and the food is consistently excellent.

Where's a good place to unwind after work? Salty's lounge, offering nautical views, tasty hor d'oeuvres, and nifty people hobnobbing at days end.

Salty's has become famous for its Halibut Supreme, Garlic Cheese Bread, and its Salads with Raspberry Vinegar Dressing, to name a few (the favorites go on and on). You'll enjoy scrumptious desserts which are prepared daily at the restaurants own bakery across the street. On Salty's front patio, you'll find a seasonal Fish and Chips Bar, offering Salty's famous Seafood Chowder etc.

For a lazy noon or evening meal, water side, drive to Salty's on the beach at Redondo.

Salty's is located at 28201 Redondo Beach Drive So., Federal Way. Call 946-0636 from Seattle or 272-0607 from Tacoma for reservations. A second location is at 1936 Harbor Avenue S.W. at Alki in Seattle. Call 937-1600 for reservations.

219

RASPBERRY VINEGAR

A LA - Salty's

1	cup frozen or fresh raspberries with juice
1-1/2	quarts white vinegar

1.   Combine ingredients.
2.   Let sit at room temperature for 24 hours.
3.   Strain and use.

Yield: 1-1/2 quarts

Raspberry Vinegar is very popular. Make this and have on hand for any recipe which calls for it.

SPINACH LEAVES WITH RASPBERRY VINEGAR DRESSING

A LA - Salty's

Raspberry Vinegar Dressing
1	**cup raspberry vinegar** (see recipe previous page)
3	**cups salad oil**
3/4	**T. salt**
1/2	**T. black pepper**
1/2	**t. granulated garlic or 1 clove fresh garlic** (minced)

1	**bunch fresh spinach** (washed, dried, torn)
1	**tomato** (cut in thin wedges)
1	**cup mushrooms** (sliced)
1/4	**cup green onion** (chopped)
1	**egg** (hard boiled and sliced)
1/4	**cup dried banana chips**

Raspberry Vinegar Dressing
1. Combine vinegar, oil, salt, pepper and garlic, Whisk until well combined.
2. In salad bowl or on individual chilled plates, arrange spinach leaves, tomatoes, mushrooms, onion, egg slices and banana chips.
3. Pour small amount of dressing. Toss gently and serve.

Serves: 2
Preparation: 15 minutes

A delicious salad. Dressing is light and perky. Banana chips are a great contrast.

GARLIC CHEESE BREAD

A LA - Salty's

1	**jumbo loaf French bread** (sliced lengthwise)
1/2	**lb. butter**
1	**T. fresh garlic** (minced)
1/4	**cup cheddar cheese** (grated)
1/4	**cup parmesan cheese** (grated)
	grated cheddar for garnish

1. Preheat oven to 450º. Warm bread in foil for 3 minutes.
2. Meanwhile, in food processor or blender combine butter, garlic and cheeses. Process to thoroughly blend.
3. Remove bread from oven and spread butter over each half.
4. Slice bread along width every 3 inches. Garnish with additional cheddar as desired.
5. Place open-faced on cookie sheet and broil for one minute or until edges are brown and serve.

Serves: 4
Preparation: 10 minutes

A real winner! Everyone loves Salty's Garlic-Cheese Bread. Perfect accompaniment to our Northwest Sea- food dishes or barbecued meat or poultry. Better make double as this is a favorite.

222

HALIBUT SUPREME WITH CHEESE DILL SAUCE

A LA - Salty's

1	lb. halibut filets
2	T. butter (melted)
1/2	cup white wine
1	t. granulated garlic
	white pepper

Cheese Dill Sauce

1	cup sour cream
1/2	cup cheddar cheese (grated)
1	T. garlic (minced)
1	T. fresh dill (minced) (or 1 t. dry)

1/2	cup bay shrimp

1. Preheat oven 450º.
2. Place filets in shallow baking pan. Add butter, white wine, garlic and white pepper.
3. Bake for 6-7 minutes or until fish flakes easily. Do not overbake.

Cheese Dill Sauce

4. Combine sour cream, cheese, garlic and dill in sauce pan over low heat.
5. Simmer until cheese melts. Keep warm.
6. Remove fish from oven; top with cheese sauce and shrimp.

Serves: 4
Preparation: 15 minutes

A must for fresh halibut! Sure to please everyone. Test kitchen highly recommended sauce for any white fish.

CHOCOLATE DIPPED STRAWBERRIES

A LA - Salty's

2	**cups semi-sweet chocolate chips or 2 cups white chocolate** (broken)
1	**T. salad oil**
1	**quart perfect strawberries** (washed and thoroughly dried, stems remaining).

1. Melt chocolate in double boiler over simmering water.
2. Thin with oil
3. Dip strawberries in chocolate, halfway up berry.
4. Lay on waxpaper covered cookie sheet.
5. Allow chocolate to harden and serve.

Serves: 4 as dessert
Preparation: 20 minutes

Always a favorite. Try some in each color for an impressive dessert tray. Can also be used to garnish other desserts. Can be made ahead and refrigerated.

Sophisticated, and strikingly designed at every turn, Simon's brings uptown class to this flourishing Southcenter hub, with its modern glass, fresh flowers, canopied courtyard, dramatic greenery, fresh flowers and soft decor. The rich, dark woods in the elegant bar exude warmth while patrons listen to classy piano music. Two beautifully appointed private dining rooms are also available and can handle large or small parties.

"Cooking without sauces is like painting without colours". The chefs at Simon's obviously agree with renowned French Chef Verge in their presentation of creative entrees.

The Roast Duckling's tangy raspberry sauce can make any poultry or veal outstanding with its wonderfully refreshing flavor.

The Salmon Noir is also excellent, prepared Cajun style. We invite you to try the recipes that follow and to use the sauces with creative abandon.

Whether entertaining a client or treating a special friend, Simon's is a special place for all occasions.

Simon's is located at 17401 Southcenter Parkway, Tukwila. Call 575-3500 for reservations.

225

BIBB SHAWNESSY

A LA - Simon's

2	heads bibb lettuce (washed and dried)
1/4	cup shredded coconut
1/2	cup mandarin oranges or fresh satsumas
1/4	cup slivered almonds (toasted)

Shawnessy Dressing (yields 1 cup)

1/8	cup red wine vinegar
1	large egg (coddled)*
1	cup salad oil
1	T. fresh minced mint (or 1 t. dry)
1	T. fresh minced basil (or 1 t. dry)
1/2	T. fresh minced oregano (or 1/2 t. dry)
1	clove garlic (minced)
1	T. lemon juice
1	T. olive oil
1	T. Dijon mustard
1	T. honey

1. Tear lettuce and place in salad bowl. Add coconut, oranges and almonds. Set aside.
2. In blender or food processer bowl, combine vinegar and egg. Process until blended. With motor running, slowly add oil in steady stream. It will thicken to mayonnaise consistency.
3. Add mint, basil, oregano and garlic. Process to incorporate. Slowly add lemon juice and olive oil and process again.
4. Season with mustard and honey. Taste and adjust seasonings.

- continued -

5.   Pour desired amount of dressing over lettuce and fruit. Toss gently and serve immediately.

Serves: 4
Preparation: 10 minutes

*To coddle egg: place in boiling water, cover pan and turn off heat. Egg will be coddled in 6-8 minutes.

A super salad. Very colorful and flavors are wonderful. We all fought for seconds so make plenty.

SIMON'S SHELLFISH CHOWDER BASE

(To be used with chowder, next page)

A LA - Simon's

1/2	**lb. butter**
1/4	**lb. bacon** (diced)
1-1/4	**cups flour**
2	**cups onion** (diced)
1/2	**bay leaf**
1	**t. salt**
2	**t. white pepper**
2	**t. ground thyme**
5	**cups clam juice** (heated)*
1	**cup Sauterne wine**
2	**cups potatoes** (diced)
2	**cups celery** (diced)

1. Melt butter in large stock pot.
2. In another pan, cook bacon until three quarters cooked, 7-8 minutes.
3. Add the bacon and drippings to melted butter. Add flour.
4. Cook for 10 minutes over medium low heat. Stir occasionally.
5. Add onion, bay leaf and spices; cook for additional 3-4 minutes.
6. Add clam juice, wine and potatoes.
7. Bring to a simmer; cook until potatoes are done.
8. Add celery; simmer 10 minutes, then turn off heat.
9. Cool and store in refrigerator up to 3 weeks or freeze.

Yields: 2-1/2 quarts
Preparation: 45 minutes

*May be purchased in canned food section of your grocery.
Keep on hand to make an easy and quick Simon's Shellfish Chowder (recipe next page).

SIMON'S SHELLFISH CHOWDER

A LA - Simon's

4	**cups chowder base** (see recipe on previous page)
2	**cups half and half** (heated)
1/4	**cup clam juice** (heated)*
1/4	**cup Sauterne wine**
1/4	**lb. bay shrimp**
1/4	**lb. scallops** (chopped)
1/4	**lb. dungeness crab meat**

1. Heat chowder base in large pot.
2. Add half and half; simmer until absorbed, 4-5 minutes.
3. Add clam juice, wine and seafood.
4. Cook until thoroughly heated (it only takes a few minutes for the seafood to cook.)

Serves: 10 as 1st course; 4 as hearty meal
Preparation: 15 minutes

*Buy canned clam juice in your local grocery store.

A good variation of N.W. chowder.

TROUT PECAN MENIERE

A LA - Simon's

Meuniere Sauce
1   **cup demi-glace** or rich beef gravy
1/2   **cup butter**
1/4   **cup worchestershire sauce**
1   **T. lemon juice**
1/4   **t. tabasco sauce**

Pecan Butter
1/2   **lb. pecans** (finely chopped)
1   **cup warm soft butter**
1/4   **cup lemon juice**
1   **T. worchestershire sauce**
1/4   **t. salt**
1/4   **t. pepper**

4   **(10 oz.) trout** (skinned and filleted)
4   **eggs** (beaten)
1/2   **cup flour**
1/2   **cup butter** (*clarified*-see Glossary)
12   **whole pecans** (for garnish)

Meuniere Sauce
1.   Combine demi-glace, butter, worchestershire sauce, lemon juice and tabasco. Bring to a boil and remove from heat. Set aside and keep hot.

- continued -

230

Pecan Butter

2. Blend pecans, soft butter, lemon juice, worchester-shire sauce and salt and pepper. Set aside.
3. Flour trout; then dip in egg and flour again.
4. Heat butter in saute pans and cook trout, browning both sides.
5. Serve with Meuniere Sauce over top garnished with one tablespoon pecan butter on top and sprinkling of pecans

Serves: 4
Preparation: 20 minutes

A Simon's favorite!

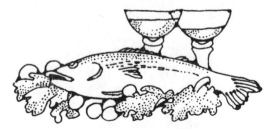

SEAFOOD SEASONING SPICE

A LA - Simon's

3	T. salt
2	T. granulated garlic
2	T. black pepper
1/2	T. cayenne pepper
1	T. whole thyme (minced)
1	T. whole oregano (minced)
3	T. paprika
1-1/2	T. granulated onion

1. Combine all ingredients.
2. Store in cool place.
3. Use for any blackened fish recipe.

Yield: 1 cup
Preparation: 3 minutes

The secret to Simon's delicious Blackened Seafood dishes. Use on *Blackened Salmon;* next page, and keep on hand for other uses.

SALMON NOIR WITH VEGETABLES

(Blackened Salmon)

A LA - Simon's

4	**(6 oz.) salmon filets**
1/2	**cup Seafood Seasoning Spice** (see recipe previous page)
2	**cups red cabbage** (thinly sliced)
1	**cup green pepper** (julienned*)
1	**cup white onion** (julienned*)
1	**cup carrot** (julienned*)
3	**T. butter**
1/2	**cup sweet butter**
1	**large lemon**

1. Preheat oven to 450º. Open windows, turn on exhaust fan.
2. Heat cast iron skillet over burner until red hot.
3. Coat filets on both sides with seafood seasoning.
4. Drop onto hot fry pan. Cook for 30 seconds on each side.
5. Place pan in oven and bake for 8 minutes.
6. In separate pan, saute vegetables to just crisp stage in 3 T. butter. Add additional Seasoning Spice to taste. Set aside.
7. In another pan melt sweet butter over low heat; add juice from lemon and heat.
8. To serve, place vegetables on plates; top with filets and pour sauce over filets.

Serves: 4
Preparation: 15 minutes

*See *Julienne* in Glossary.

Flavors are wonderful. Color contrast is eye-catching and fish is moist.

ROAST DUCKLING WITH RASPBERRY SAUCE

A LA - Simon's

4-5	lb. duck
3	t. honey
	salt and pepper
1/4	cup flour
1/2	cup carrots (chopped)
1/2	cup celery (chopped)
1/4	cup onion (chopped)
2	cups fresh or frozen raspberries
1/2	cup raspberry wine vinegar*
1	shallot (diced)
1	T. honey
2	T. cornstarch
2	kiwi fruit (sliced-garnish)
	fresh raspberries (garnish)

1. Preheat oven to 275º. Rub duck with honey; season with salt and pepper. Lightly coat with flour.
2. Bake in shallow pan 2-1/2 to 3 hours or until brown.
3. Remove and let cool for 1 hour.
4. De-bone duck by splitting down middle from breast bone to tail. Keep meat intact.
5. Put bones and fat in boiling water to cover. Add carrots, celery and onion. Cook for at least 1 hour at a simmer..
6. Strain. Discard vegetables. Cook and reduce liquid to almost nothing.
7. Add raspberries to essence along with 1-1/2 cups water, 1/2 cup raspberry vinegar and shallot.
8. Reduce by half by cooking and strain through mesh colander. Push some raspberry meat through.

- continued -

234

9.   Add honey and cornstarch mixed with 1/4 cup water.
        Stir until thickened. Keep warm.
10.   Reheat duck in 350º oven for 10 minutes until skin is
        crisp and golden brown.
11.   Serve duck cut in half; topped with sauce; garnished
        with kiwi slices and fresh berries.

Serves: 2 (with sauce left over)
Preparation: 2 hours (includes 1 hour cook time.)
Baking: 3 hours

*Either purchase in store or make your own. See index,
Raspberry Vinegar (Salty's) for recipe.

Chef says this is a true specialty often requested by return
patrons. Can be done in 2 steps to cut down on preparation.
Cook duck and stock one day. Make sauce and finish just
before serving.

**A delicious sauce equally good over chicken or game
hens.**

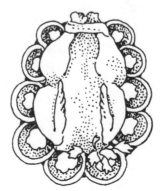

SESAME CHICKEN APPETIZER

A LA - Simon's

1-1/2	**cups cornstarch**
1-1/2	**cups flour**
2	**cups water**
1/2	**cup rice vinegar**
1/3	**cup soy sauce**
1/3	**cup sesame oil**
2	**t. ground ginger**
2	**t. granulated garlic**
1	**lb. boneless, skinless chicken breasts** (cut in strips)
2-3	**cups vegetable oil** (for deep frying chicken)
	sesame seeds

1. Combine cornstarch and flour.
2. Slowly add water, stirring until mixture is well blended.
3. Add vinegar, soy sauce, sesame oil, ginger and garlic.
4. Dip chicken in batter until thoroughly covered.
5. Deep fry in hot oil until golden brown. Watch closely because chicken cooks quickly.
6. Serve with sesame seeds and favorite dip such as a hot mustard etc.

Serves: 4-6 as appetizer
Preparation: 10-15 minutes

Good 1st course!

SPACE NEEDLE

The Space Needle is fast becoming as famous for its food as for its landmark status and panorama. The motto, "Good Food, Above All Else" rings truer than ever in the space age shaped tower, commanding a 360º view from its revolving restaurant.

Like its French cousin, the Eiffel Tower, the Space Needle remains as a symbol of a world's fair and still features exhibits at the observation level, 20 feet above the restaurant.

We are delighted at the change in recent years giving us not just one but two restaurants in one. There is the curtained-off, elegant Emerald Suite with its nouvelle cuisine, touting only the freshest Northwest fare, and the Space Needle Restaurant, specializing in Pacific Salmon and fresh local bounty. Both revolve at the 500 foot level, to give you a spectacular view as you dine.

Every gem in the city's Emerald crown sparkles as you dine; the Puget Sound, Olympic and Cascade Mountains, Lake Union and downtown Seattle.

- continued -

There are wonderful specialties such as Seattle Stew, and Salmon served in a variety of ways: stuffed, marinated with fresh lime and dill or with lime and tumeric. Oysters, clams, mussels, dungeness crab and hand-picked fruits and vegetables grace your table, fresh from the Pike Place Market.

The service deserves an entire page by itself to laud the genuine friendliness and jovial nature of all Space Needle employees, from the receptionist at ground level to the bartender above. And while you overlook everything, talented chefs and servers overlook nothing in providing you the best of the Northwest's cuisine. Definitely worth mentioning is the skyline banquet facility, offering superb cuisine and a terrific view for parties large or small. The newly refurbished Top of the Needle Lounge is better than ever.

We heartily agree with one restaurant critic who noted, "There is no longer any need to wait for an out-of-town visitor to justify dining at this Space Needle." Reservations are highly recommended for breakfast, lunch or dinner.

Located at the Seattle Center Space Needle.
Call 443-2100 for reservations.

238

SPIRIT OF THE NEEDLE

A LA - Space Needle

1/2	**oz. rum**
1/2	**oz. Amaretto**
1/2	**oz. orange juice**
1/2	**oz. half and half**
1/2	**oz. sweet and sour mix** *or* margarita mix
1/2	**cup fresh strawberries**
1/4	**cup ice**

1. Combine all ingredients in blender.
2. Process until smooth.
3. Serve in brandy snifter or balloon glass.

Serves: 1
Preparation: 2 minutes

Delicious smooth drink!

OYSTERS AU GRATIN WITH PERNOD

A LA - Space Needle

6	**medium oysters** (shucked*, reserving 6 nice half-shells)
1/4	**cup cheddar cheese**
1/4	**cup gruyere cheese**
2	**T. parmesan cheese**
6	**fresh spinach leaves**
2	**T. Pernod liqueur**
1	**tomato** (finely diced; divided into 6 portions)

1. Preheat oven to 350º.
2. Drain oysters and place one on each half-shell.
3. Combine 3 cheeses; mix well.
4. Top each oyster with spinach leaf, some of cheese mixture and dash of Pernod.
5. Garnish each with diced tomato.
6. Bake in oven for 8 minutes. Serve immediately.

Serves: 2 as appetizer
Preparation: 10 minutes

*See Glossary for *shucked.*

A good way to begin any meal.

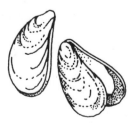

COQUILLES ST. JACQUES
Seafood in Creamy Cheese Casserole

A LA - Space Needle

1/2	**lb. scallops**
1/4	**lb. shrimp meats**
1/4	**cup flour**
3	**T. butter**
1/4	**lb. crabmeat**
1	**cup mushrooms** (sliced)
3/4	**cup cream**
1/2	**lb. montorey jack cheese** (shredded)

1. Preheat oven to broil. Dust scallops and shrimp with flour. Shake off excess.
2. Melt butter in saute pan. Add scallops, shrimp, crab and mushrooms.
3. Cook for 3-4 minutes.
4. Pour in cream; bring to boil. Cook until cream is reduced and forms a sauce. This takes 3-4 minutes.
5. Divide mixture into 4 individual casserole dishes or oven proof scallop shells.
6. Top with shredded cheese. Broil until cheese bubbles and browns.

Serves: 4
Preparation: 15 minutes

A sure hit with all seafood lovers! The flavors combine beautifully and presentation is impressive.

BAKED APPLE WITH VANILLA SAUCE

A LA - Space Needle

4	**small red rome apples** (cored) (or other small apple suitable for baking)
1/4	**cup walnuts** (chopped)
1/4	**cup granulated sugar**
1/2	**cup brown sugar**
4	**4" by 4" sheets of puff pastry***
1	**T. sugar** (garnish)
4	**cinnamon sticks**

Vanilla Sauce

1	**cup cream**
3	**T. sugar**
1/2	**t. vanilla extract**
1	**t. cornstarch mixed with 2 t. water**

1. Preheat oven to 325º / 350º.
2. Mix together walnuts and brown and white sugar.
3. Stuff cored apples with sugar-walnut mixture.
4. Place apples in centers of puff pastry squares.
5. Fold pastry around apple completely encasing apple.
6. Sprinkle pastry with remaining sugar (1 T.) and insert cinnamon stick 1/4" down into core.
7. Bake until pastry turns a light brown and puffs (10-20 minutes depending on your oven.

- continued -

242

Vanilla Sauce

8. Bring cream, sugar and vanilla to a slow boil over medium heat. Do not burn.
9. Add cornstarch mixed with water and cook 3 minutes on simmer or until thickened.
10. Remove apples from oven; place on dessert plates and serve warm sauce over top.

Serves: 4
Preparation: 20 minutes

*Ask your bakery for them or purchase Fillo Leaves in frozen food section of your local grocery store.

Test kitchen found this to be a very pleasing dessert to both palate and eyes.
Sauce would be delicious over any fruit pie or cobbler.

13 Coins

As a stranger to saltwater and Seattle many years ago, 13 Coins was one of the first gourmet restaurants recommended to me by a trusted friend for its wonderfully delicious Italian food, and its generous portions.

It is one of Seattle's most popular late-night spots, open 24 hours, seven days a week. I'm not the last of the midnight snackers to appreciate this because I've always had plenty of company even after 1 a.m. when visions of Veal Antipasto or French Onion Soup draw me there after theater or dancing. If you get a hankering to bite into a juicy steak or just nestle in high-backed seats to watch expert chefs flip omelets in the open galley, this is the place for it.

Robert Joffrey of the Joffrey Ballet Company never leaves Seattle without having relished the Coins Steak Sinatra after dance performances. (The recipe follows; be sure to try it.)

Look for the Coin Medallion above the door and you'll find excellent continental cuisine awaiting you.

13 Coins is located at 125 Boren Avenue, across from the Seattle Times Building, with another near Sea-Tac Airport. For reservations call 682-2513 (Boren) or 243-9500 (Sea-Tac).

JOE'S SPECIAL

A LA - 13 Coins

1	**cup onions** (chopped)
2	**T. olive oil**
1	**lb. ground round**
1	**t. seasoning salt**
1	**cup chopped spinach** (squeezed dry)
6	**whole eggs**
1/4	**cup grated asiago cheese***
1/4	**cup grated parmesan**

1. Saute onions in olive oil over medium high heat.
2. Add ground round and season with salt.
3. Cook until medium well. Break up with fork.
4. Add spinach and whole eggs and stir and cook until done, but not dry.
5. Serve on individual plates. Sprinkle with combined cheeses.

Serves: 4
Preparation: 10 minutes

*You can substitute romano cheese if you desire.

Seattle's favorite version of this classic dish. Chef says try a variation using 1 cup mushrooms. Garnish with 1-1/2 tablespoons of sour cream and green onions. 13 Coins calls this dish, Ukranian Joe.

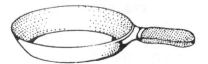

SEAFOOD FRITTATA

A LA - 13 Coins

2	**T. oil**
4	**scallops**
2	**prawns** (cut in thirds)
1/2	**cup onion** (chopped)
1/2	**cup mushrooms** (sliced)
1/2	**cup shrimp**
8	**large eggs** (beaten)
1/4	**cup asiago cheese** *(freshly grated)
1/4	**cup parmesan** (freshly grated)

1. Preheat oven 350º.
2. In saute pan, heat oil and saute scallops and prawns until almost done (a few minutes).
3. Add onion and mushrooms; cook until done.
4. Combine eggs and shrimp meat.
5. Add to saute pan and cook until underside is done.
6. Bake until top side is cooked, but not dry. Frittata should be golden brown.
7. Remove from oven; slide onto serving platter.
8. Sprinkle with cheeses and serve.

Serves: 2-4
Preparation: 15-20 minutes

*You can substitute romano cheese if you desire.

A 13 Coins classic. Try for brunch or light supper! Another version of the above uses bacon, onion, zucchini and spinach in place of seafood.

FETTUCCINE VENETIA

A LA - 13 Coins

6-8	**scallops** (depending on size)
4	**prawns** (cut lengthwise in 3 pieces each, shelled and deveined)
1	**cup mushrooms (quartered)**
1/2	**cup butter**
4	**cups cooked fettuccine**
4	**egg yolks**
2	**cups half & half**
1	**cup small cooked shrimp**
1/2	**cup asiago or romano cheese** (grated)
1/2	**cup parmesan cheese** (grated)

1. Cook scallops, prawns and mushrooms in butter slowly. Do not brown butter.
2. Add fettuccine, half & half, egg yolks and shrimp.
3. In separate bowl, mix together asiago and parmesan cheeses. Add to the scallops.
4. Cook until sauce begins to form. Remove from heat and serve.

Serves: 4
Preparation: 15 minutes

A lightly seasoned seafood dish. Perfect for a light meal with green salad and sourdough bread - or as a first course.

FETTUCCINE ALLA BURRO DOLCE
(Fettuccine with Sweet Butter Sauce)

A LA - 13 Coins

6	**cups cooked fettuccine**
1/2	**cup butter**
2	**cups half & half**
4	**egg yolks**
	salt and pepper (to taste)
1/2	**cup asiago or romano cheese** (grated)
1/2	**cup parmesan** (grated)
2	**T. chopped parsley** (garnish)

1. In a medium pan melt butter, add cooked fettuccine, half & half, egg yolks, salt and pepper.
2. Cook until sauce begins to form. Mix asiago and parmesan cheeses together and add to the sauce.
3. Garnish with parsley and serve immediately.

Serves: 4
Preparation: 10 minutes

A wonderful accompaniment to chicken or meat.

STEAK SINATRA

A LA - 13 Coins

4	**(4 oz.) tenderloins** (sliced into 3 pieces each)
1-1/2	**T. oil**
1	**whole onion** (cut into 12ths)
1	**whole green pepper** (cut into 12ths)
10	**whole button mushrooms**
	salt and pepper
1	**clove garlic** (minced)
2	**artichoke hearts** (cut in halves)
1	**tomato** (cut in 8ths)
1/4	**cup burgundy wine**

1. Sear meat, in hot oil, on both sides.
2. Add onion, peppers, mushrooms, salt, pepper and garlic.
3. Saute until still crisp but lightly cooked.
4. Add artichoke hearts, tomatoes and burgundy wine. Cook 2-3 minutes more.
5. Drain off 3/4 of liquid and serve immediately.

Serves: 4
Preparation: 10 minutes

A perfect and very popular stir-fry dish. Great with French Fries!

BERRIES IN CHANTILLY CREAM

A LA - 13 Coins

1	**cup whipping cream** (whipped)
3/4	**cup brown sugar**
2/3	**cup sour cream**
1	**T. Grand Marnier**
	Fresh berries such as;

> strawberries
> raspberries
> blackberries

1. Combine whipped cream, sugar, sour cream and Grand Marnier.
2. Layer with berries in parfait glasses.
3. Serve immediately.

Serves: 4-6
Preparation: 5 minutes

A perfect sauce for seasonal berries or fruit.

GLOSSARY OF TERMS

Al Dente

Cooked until tender but not soft; 5 - 10 minutes. Home-made noodles, 5 minutes; if on shelf for long period, 8 - 10 minutes. Literally in Italian this means "to the tooth". In other words, it resists your bite slightly.

Bearnaise Sauce

This is a Hollandaise Sauce flavored with Tarragon, Shallots and Wine. You can add those ingredients to your Hollandaise or follow the recipe here:

5 egg yolks (large) 3 T. lemon juice, salt and pepper to taste, 3 T. shallots (minced) 2 T. wine vinegar, 1½ T. dried tarragon, 1½ cups butter (melted) ¼ t. tabasco - Combine yolks, lemon juice and salt and pepper in top of double boiler over gently simmering water. Whip together with whisk until sauce begins to thicken. In separate pan, simmer shallots, vinegar and tarragon for three minutes. Slowly add to yolk mixture. Reduce heat and very slowly add melted butter, drop by drop, all the while beating the sauce with electric beater until sauce is consistency of Hollandaise. Finally, add tabasco.

Bordelaise Sauce

Prepare the same way you do BROWN SAUCE except in addition to the onion, saute also ½ carrot (sliced), a few slices of celery, a sprig of parsley and ½ bay leaf (crushed). Add 1 T. of ketchup or tomato puree and if you desire, a dash of worcestershire and dry red wine. If you use packaged gravy, simply add 1 T. catsup and a dash of worcestershire sauce.

Brown Sauce

You may use packaged Beef Gravy Sauce or make your own. The following is a very simple recipe using ingredients you most likely have on hand:

Saute 1 T. of diced onion in 2 T. of butter. Add 2 T. flour to make a roux. Stir in 1 cup of consomme or beef bouillon and salt and pepper to taste. Cook over low heat, stirring constantly, or cook in a double boiler. Strain. Yields 1 cup.

Butterfly

To Butterfly Shrimp: Remove shell but leave tail intact. Devein. Turn upside down and cut all the way down length of shrimp to tail and almost all the way through to other side. (leave about 1/16

— Continued —

GLOSSARY OF TERMS - Continued

inch to act as a hinge). Spread shrimp open butterfly fashion and lay flat. It will resemble the shape of a butterfly.

For other meats: Slicing against or across the grain to make it more tender. Also, to open up a pocket for stuffing by cutting through the middle of the side of a filet and opening up two flaps which can later enclose stuffing.

Clarified, Clarify

To make clear by adding a clarifying agent or removing sediment. In the case of butter, simply melt it over low heat. In between the foam on top and the milk solids which will have settled to the bottom of your pan, you will have a clear liquid. This is your clarified butter. Skim the foam from the top and discard. Tilt pan to gather your clarified butter. The sediment at the bottom can be discarded or used in baking if you desire.

Creme Fraiche

To make this slightly soured cream, you add 1 T. buttermilk to 1 cup heavy cream. Let sit in warm place overnight - or about 15 - 20 hours. In some cases you may substitute heavy cream.

Correct the Seasonings

Add salt and pepper to taste

Demi-Glace

A reduced Brown Sauce. For a quick Demi-Glace, simply cook brown gravy 15 - 20 minutes until flavors are concentrated. You can use a packaged gravy.

Deglaze

To moisten a roast pan or saute pan with wine, vinegar, stock or water in order to dissolve the carmelized drippings from roasted meats, etc., so that they might be used in the sauce. To do this, scrape up the bottom residue into the liquid with a wooden spatula while cooking over low heat.

Dressed

Stuffed.

Fish Stock

Add ½ cup each of sliced onion, carrot and celery to 3 cups cold water and ½ cup white wine. Bring to a boil and add 1 lb. of fish bones, head, tails, trimmings, etc. Cook for twenty minutes and strain. In some cases you may substitute chicken stock or bouillon.

— Continued —

253

Flamber or Flambe

This process adds flavor to dessert and meat dishes. Light match to warmed liqueur to make a flame and burn off the alcohol. It's easy to ignite if you tilt the pan and touch the flame to the edge. It will burn itself out.

Flour (Browned)

This is great for gravies and sauce as it enhances the flavor. Simply brown the amount of flour you need in a cast iron skillet or other heavy pan, stirring constantly. Be sure the flour does not get too brown. It should be golden brown in color. An alternate method is to brown it in a moderate oven for 20 - 30 minutes till golden, stirring occasionally.

Garlic (Pressed)

Use a garlic press to squeeze out the juice and pulverize the clove. Discard the hull. If you do not own a press, you may mash the garlic with the blade of a knife or with the back of a spoon against the side of the bowl you are using.

Ignite

See Flamber

Julienne

To cut in long thin 1½ inch strips. Should be thinner than French fries.

Lump Crab Meat

Lump crab meat or back-fin meat is taken from the body of the blue crabs. It is white in color. You may use just about any kind of crab for most of the recipes included in this book. While doing so, however, it's interesting to keep notes on the difference in color, taste and even the texture. Claw meat, for example, is harder to shell and is brownish in color but is very tasty.

Puff Pastry

A light puffy pastry dough. Since this requires a lot of time and perfect conditions to make, we suggest you purchase it in your grocer's bakery section. It's best to go in early or call the day before and reserve some. You can also use frozen dough for puff pastries such as croissant dough. After the dough has reached room temperature, roll it into flat rectangular shape as called for in the recipes of this book.

— Continued —

254

GLOSSARY OF TERMS - Continued

Reduce

To reduce the quantity of a liquid by simmering. This makes a stock or sauce more flavorful because it's more concentrated and is thickened.

Roux

Equal parts of flour and butter cooked - used to thicken sauces and gravies. (Melt butter over low heat. Stir in flour and cook over low heat for 1 - 2 minutes, until mixture is thick and well blended).

Saute

To cook quickly in small amount of fat or butter.

Seasonings

(Adjust or Correct) To make sure seasonings (salt and pepper, etc.) are correct to the taste - your taste. Add more if necessary.

Shuck

(Noun) - A husk, shell or pod. A shell of an oyster or clam. (Verb) - To remove shell of oyster or clam. You can do this by prying shell hinge open with knife and then inserting knife all around edge or place shells in hot oven for 5 minutes and drop in ice bath. Drain. Shells will open.

Sweetbreads

The pancreas of beef and veal. Use veal sweetbreads in all the recipes in this book. Make sure they are very fresh.

Vinaigrette Dressing Recipe

The proportions are usually 4 parts oil to 1 part lemon or lime juice or vinegar. Add herbs, spices and seasonings as you like. Here is one version: 1 tsp. salt, pinch of paprika, pinch of dry mustard, 2 T. vinegar, 8 T. olive oil, pinch of fresh ground pepper and ¼ tsp. of chopped parsley. Mix together thoroughly and serve.

Zest

The grated peelings from citrus fruits which add wonderful flavors. Avoid the white portion attached to the peel as it is bitter.

CATEGORY INDEX

Exact Recipe Titles Under Course Categories.

APPETIZERS AND HORS D'OEUVRES
(Several Entrees can also be used as Appetizers - See Entrees)

GENERAL

SEAFOOD

SALADS

CATEGORY INDEX

257

CATEGORY INDEX

CATEGORY INDEX

DESSERT

CATEGORY INDEX

Dear Friends,

Would you like us to send you other books in our series? Or send them as gift(s) to your friend(s)? We mail promptly and guarantee satisfaction!

Thank you for your order, and remember, we always appreciate your comments.

FREE SHIPPING ON FOUR BOOKS OR MORE!

Qty.	Title	Unit Price		Shipping	Total
	A LA SEATTLE	$11.95	soft cover	$1.50 ea.	
	A LA NEW ORLEANS	$11.95	soft cover	$1.50 ea.	
	A LA SAN FRANCISCO	$11.95	soft cover	$1.50 ea.	
	A LA ASPEN	$11.95	soft cover	$1.50 ea.	
	A LA TEXAS	$14.95	hard cover	$2.00 ea.	
	SEATTLE APRON	$12.00		$1.50 ea.	
	Washington Residents add 8.1% Sales Tax				
	(PRICES SUBJECT TO CHANGE) Total Enclosed				

Name _____

Address_____

City _____ State_____ Zip_____

☐ This is a gift. Send directly to: ☐ Please gift wrap (no charge)

Name _____

Address_____

City _____ State_____ Zip_____

Crabtree Publishing
P.O. Box 3451
Federal Way, WA 98063

Other books will soon be available. Please check the titles that interest you, or let us know which books you might like to see.

Thank you.

A La - San Diego / La Jolla _____

A La - Santa Fe _____

A La - Cape Cod _____

A La - Majorca, Spain _____

A La - Chicago _____

A La - Los Angeles _____

A La - Manhattan _____

A La - _____

A La - _____

A La - _____